EVER Near

A Series of Love Letters Between Soulmates,
Transcending our Understanding of Life and Death

Tim Bair

FRANKLIN ROSE
PUBLISHING

Publisher: Franklin Rose, Inc.

www.FranklinRose.com

ISBN: 978-1-952146-26-8 (Paperback)

ISBN: 978-1-952146-27-5 (eBook)

Library of Congress Control Number: 2023911785

Contents

To our six children and thirteen grandchildren:
We want you to know that everything we have done in life
has been for you. You are the reason for our every action,
and we love you more than words can express.

To Jennifer Shaffer:
Your unparalleled skills as a psychic medium have been
instrumental in helping me communicate with my Eternal
Love. From the moment we met, you encouraged me to
begin writing from Spirit, and without your guidance, our
story would never have been told. I am eternally grateful for
your support. (Jennifershaffer.com)

To DeEtte:
Your mentorship has been a guiding light in my life. You
have challenged me to step outside of my comfort zone and
explore new horizons. Your cherished friendship, support,
and vision have given me the courage to continue reaching
for what lies beyond my own sight. (deEtte.Us)

To Richard Martini:

Your books, films, and podcasts have been a source of inspiration and comfort, helping me realize that I am not alone in my experiences. Your work helped create a foundation for me to stand on as I began my own journey. I highly recommend your extensive body of work to anyone seeking answers about the afterlife. (richmartini.com, hackingtheafterlife.quora.com)

To Elaine Kravits-Sheppard:

I cannot express enough gratitude for your invaluable contribution to this work. Without your expert editing skills, this would have been a jumbled collection of poorly punctuated stories. Your dedication and attention to detail have transformed this project.

Forward

Some years ago, Tim reached out to me to share an extraordinary experience. He had lost his wife Mari Lynn and had been trying to communicate with her on the other side until one day when he felt her take his arm while he was going for a walk. He could hear her voice, feel her touch, which led to these series of letters that he sat down to write, and heard her responses.

When looking into stories about the Flipside, I try to focus on those that are consistent and reproducible, or more than one person reports the same things. Mari Lynn reports many of the same things about the Flipside those in the research report.

That they are not gone, they need to wait until we get to an emotional equilibrium so we can hear them. Not everyone can, but it requires effort, patience, and lowering one's filters. (Which helps when someone is "automatic writing.")

These letters from the Flipside are a testament to a great love story, and the fact that Tim has put them into book form will allow others to be healed and helped by them.

I highly recommend taking the time to read Ever Near, Tim and Mari Lynn's story, which is ongoing and contains qualities of unconditional love and eternal beauty. She's not gone; she's just not here.

Richard Martini Best-selling author of "Flipside" "Divine Councils in the Afterlife"

My Dearest Love,

It took us several years to put into words what happened that day when a completely new reality exploded in us. Yes, it felt new but at the same time, it was old, ancient, and comfortable. Safe in ways we instantly knew nothing would be able to come between us. Now, in this moment that ancient safety is the ground we stand on. It is lifetimes of togetherness that allow this comfort to reach across time and space. We have now learned that nothing, not even the death of my body, can come between us. These mornings are very special; when you intentionally focus and write of my love for you. But the most precious thing to me is the moment-to-moment time we share.

Your Eternal Love

Introduction

Years ago, when Mari Lynn and I first were married, trouble swirled around us like some great storm, an epic hurricane, really. Our friends saw how we were able to handle everything from divorces, child support, bankruptcies, and even death threats. No matter what difficulty found us, we always were able to put one foot in front of the other and were drawn even closer together. There were always crazy circumstances that just seemed to work out. Miracles were normal for us.

Our friends saw what we were going through, marveled at what love could accomplish, and begged us to write a book. The problem was, we knew our side of the story could hurt many of the ones we loved so no book.

After Mari Lynn passed away, I found her. In quiet moments, I actually began hearing her voice. The quieter I got, the easier it was, and the more I heard. When I would sense her presence, I would feel compelled to get outside, and that's where in the quietness of 2:00 to 4:00 a.m., I talked to my eternal love. I would rush to get there. Very soon, we began to have conversations I didn't want to forget, so I began to write them down.

I tried to maintain our home, but my physical pain (from a severe injury) worsened, and my early morning walks became increasingly difficult, and was forced to make a decision I dreaded. Even though it broke my heart, I implemented our plan (one we made before, then discussed after her physical death); sell our forever home and move to the slower pace of Palm Springs. The move took a substantial toll; I was having trouble just walking to the kitchen—and I was afraid I had lost Mari Lynn forever. Long, quiet walks were out of the question. I was feeling bereft as though I was lost at sea, until I found that I could simply quiet my mind and still have the same conversations here that we had before.

One morning the irresistible feeling was back, strong and persuasive. This time instead of " Get outside and go for a walk", it demanded "Go sit down! Get a pen and paper". I never fancied myself a writer and certainly never considered writing a book by myself. Words did not come easy to me, but soon I discovered that Mari Lynn and I could connect on yet an entirely new plane.

I soon learned to get my own mind out of the way, not judge what I thought I should write, and would begin to write a sentence without knowing the thought behind it. After writing four or five pages and not having any idea where it was going, I read back conversations that gave me the joy I had only known when she was physically with me.

Now our time together is just as real as it ever was. My days are filled with discussions as we talk about anything and everything. We tell jokes, worry about our grandkids, and work around our small property we live on TOGETHER. The only real difference is she's not driving me around or handing me tools. In the still of the early morning (or any time I want), I can pick up a pen and blank piece of paper, and she will write to me.

I'm sure there are those who are cynical and won't believe it's my dead wife guiding my mind and hands, but those people have never met us. Even if you don't believe this sort of thing is possible, if you had ever been in the same room as us you would believe that if anyone could reach across eternal time and space it would be the two of us. So what you see in the following pages is the book our friends asked us to write more than 20 years ago—sort of.

I really tried to write our story in chronological order, but it was confusing even to me, and I know it. In the three or four years that Mari Lynn and I knew each other as friends, we were constantly on a journey to be together. It was a journey I did everything I could to deny, but one she spent in quiet hopefulness. Throughout those four years and the 22 years that followed, we faced incredible challenges and simultaneously experienced the deepest joy. As I said, I was going to write our story and our experiences sequentially, but many of our challenges started, stopped, and started again several years later. With situations stuttering across our entire time together, I would need to color code a spreadsheet with the "big box" of crayons neither of us could afford as children.

This book is a small part of our story, and there is so much more. It was difficult to decide what stories and "letters" to include or what should be saved for a later time.

This account may also seem one sided. Many of the situations we found ourselves in did involve people who aligned themselves against us. Naturally, our perspective is the only lens through which I can share our view.

We'll leave it to others to describe and discuss how the afterlife works. I am not an expert in this field. This book is only based on our personal experiences. I hope you can hear Mari Lynn's voice in the following pages. More than that, my only wish is that you get a sense of how much joy we experienced, even though our most difficult challenges.

If what she has to say in one letter doesn't resonate, read the next. You may find that a paragraph or sentence speaks to you. Even if you believe I've made this whole story up as a way to bypass the grief that comes from losing the person who walked with me through life's storms, you may just find the smallest hope that life and love extend beyond death.

For the most part, I've transcribed them exactly as they were written. (I may have removed a deeply personal sentence or two. If I do, I'll make a note of that.) Mari Lynn's words are in a *different font*. If I butt in or have an observation it will be in normal text. This work contains only a small fraction of the letters Mari Lynn has written to me, through me.

We both really hope you can see that love reaches beyond space and time exceeding the boundaries of eternity. And that our loved ones who seem so far away are *Ever Near*.

Our full story is one of waiting for love, finding it, letting the universe see its fullness, and then never losing it

(October 13, 2022)

PART 1
(Before)

1

My Story Before

I suppose the first question to answer in telling my story is, "How does a mountain boy get from the northern most part of California to a church classroom in the high desert of Southern California some 30 years later at exactly the right moment?" Until I started writing this book, I hadn't even thought *that* journey was important at all. But there are some parts of my childhood that help explain why I was so unable to recognize the other half of me when the universe was trying to pry my eyes open.

I was raised not just poor, but told that it was impossible for me to be anything else. My earliest memories are of being three-years-old and living in the "Mill housing". It was called that because, well, it was the low rent housing available to workers at the local sawmill in Orleans, California. The men in our small mountain community were either loggers or sawmill employees. I don't think I knew a single man who had all his fingers. That's not a joke. Saws and chainsaws don't mix very well with working as fast as you can, and food on the table was far more important than personal safety. I was in training for the logging lifestyle. By the time I was four-years-old, one of my chores was cutting kindling and helping my older brother carry it and the firewood into our house. Our only heat was a single fireplace that my dad tried to keep burning all night.

My parents were extremely strict. I was just five genera-tions removed from the origins of the Seventh Day Adventist (SDA) Church. Even though my parents were raising me with all the rules and restrictions of the church that my three times great grandparents helped found, they didn't teach me any of the faith that was supposed to be part of it. Every teacher and church leader told me that certain behaviors were sins and if not forgiven, would lead me to eternal sepa-ration from God, then I would go home and be instructed to *do* some of those exact things.

Even with that confusion, my early childhood memories are positive. I spent every moment outside I could. The only outside rules were, "Don't fight with your brothers and come home when you hear dad's whistle, or dark whichever comes first."

As a three-year-old I would climb trees much higher than my parents thought I should. I spent vast amounts of time watching clouds and playing in mud puddles and dirt. It seemed like every part of outside was talking to me; I wasn't climbing trees, I was spending time with my friends. The clouds seemed to be dancing and boiling into beautiful shapes just for me. The mud puddles were full of wonder that only my imagination could see.

Like I said, my parents were strict, and I often felt a quick swat on the behind (just saying the word, "butt", would get it hit) or a real spanking. We were never beaten, but my mom would use a ruler to keep her hand from feeling a pain that was supposed to be just for us kids. At the dinner table my dad's favorite way to keep three young boys in line was a quick thump to the temple. It got to the point that if he reached for the saltshaker, three boys would duck under the table.

As an adult looking back, I know my parents loved me, but to this day, even though I'm sure they did, I can't remember my mom reading to me or either of them telling me they loved me. I was brought up with the same parenting techniques used during the Civil War era. If love was there, it wasn't talked about or ever displayed. Even with the parenting and religious weirdness, I was having a fantastic childhood that was filled with my own imagination, until I turned six-years-old and went to school.

The school was a single room in a new building next to the very small SDA church we attended. It had two teachers, a husband-and-wife team. My first-grade teacher also taught several third and fourth graders. Her husband taught fifth through tenth grades. I was the only first grader and the following year the only second grader. My well-meaning teacher, who I dearly loved, began telling me to forget the things "I made up from outside". The hours by myself in a world of imagination were being replaced with structure and conformity. The round contours of who I was were being systematically trimmed to fit the square life my parents and church were setting before me.

Just as I was confused, shifting from a life of imagination to one of concrete structure, my dad seemed to be having similar challenges. As soon as an opportunity presented itself, he left the confines of the sawmill to work in the woods for a small logging company owned by three church members. The change would allow him to be outside. It was physical work with long hours. He came home exhausted, but somehow was happier. My dad seemed to be more at peace with himself the more he was outdoors.

The area of the forest he worked in was most often two or three hours away from home. In the summer my dad would shorten his commute by building a camp for us nearby. He would use the logging company's Caterpillar tractor to level off a campsite next to a creek he had dammed. We would live in the woods for the entire summer. My two brothers and I spent time hiking, fishing, and swimming. The three of us slept in sleeping bags on army cots behind the tent where my mom, dad, and little sister slept. For ten weeks out of the year, my life of imagination was allowed to return.

While the sawmill was year around employment, working in the woods wasn't possible in the rainy and snowy mountain winters. My dad realized that he didn't want to be in an industry where he spent four months a year unemployed, and the dismemberment and death rate was statistically high. Instead, he decided to take a computer system correspondence course (the 1960's version of online classes). He hoped to get a job where winter weather and possible death on the job wasn't a factor. I can remember him sitting at the camp table studying by lantern light.

He did get a job out of the logging industry and in my fourth-grade year, we moved to Portland Oregon where I attended a large SDA school of over 400 students in grades one through eight. I went from a class of just me, to a classroom of about 25 kids. I felt lost in this large school and there was more pressure to become something I was not. I barely had passing grades, and while I did make friends and liked being with them, being at school was becoming a horrifying place where I was often told I wasn't adequate.

For high school I was supposed to go to Laurel Wood Academy, an SDA boarding school about 70 miles from Portland where I was a legacy student. My great-great-great grandparents (who had come to Oregon in covered wagons) donated the land and the dairy farm that helped support the school, to the SDA church to found the school. My great-grandfather still lived on the family farm nearby, while my grandfather's aunts and uncles lived in the village close to the school.

About three weeks into the first school year, my high school plans were interrupted one evening when my mom called. My dad had accepted a job offer at Kettering Medical Center, another SDA institution in Ohio. They gave me the choice to stay in Oregon or move to Ohio. I chose to move. The next morning, I looked at a map and was shocked to see how far I was moving.

Unfortunately, school in Ohio was just as challenging. I did make friends, but I struggled to keep passing grades. I graduated from Spring Valley Academy in 1978. I had spent every day from the first day of first grade until the last day of 12th grade in the SDA school system.

The year, 1978, was a crazy time for me. My girlfriend, (Donna) and I graduated; I entered the nursing program at Kettering College of Medical Arts (*another* SDA school); we got pregnant; we got married; I quit college and got a job in a local machine shop. In 1979, we had our first child while living in my parents' house. Within a few months, we were able to find an apartment. Life was financially and emotionally stressed and difficult. In spite of marital issues, 13 months after our first, we had our second child.

While I was literally working my fingers to the bone at the machine shop, (my 60-year-old-fingers show the proof) my young wife was convinced that children did not cost any money to raise, a*nd* she wanted more! It was something we argued about constantly over evening meals that consisted of boxed macaroni and cheese or soup. As our second child reached her third birthday, Donna's pressure on me to have more children was increasing and the arguments over whether we could afford more mouths to feed intensified. The disagreement was temporarily resolved when she became pregnant with our third child.

My parents, who had moved several times were now in Glendale California. One evening my mom called and I could tell that something was upsetting her. It took a while, but she finally told me my dad was planning to leave their 30-year marriage. I thought that if I moved my family to Glendale, I might be able to help—unfortunately, I was wrong.

The day Donna and I drove our moving van into town, my dad moved out. It's not that I didn't understand why he left. From my perspective their relationship never seemed to be a loving one, but my mom was devastated. I was now living in a two-bedroom apartment with Donna, three young children, and my mom who was spending most of her time curled up sobbing, AND I had no job. Welcome to California!

Long story short, I found employment at a local computer retail store in Pasadena. My dad's performance declined, and he was about to be fired from his job, but he accepted a position in New Jersey instead and moved. Donna and I moved into a small two-bedroom home and had our fourth child. Fortunately, my mom found a wonderful man who truly loved her, and life was definitely looking up.

I was now living in La Crescenta, near Glendale California, working as the manager of the computer store. It was a great place to live. In about an hour we could be at the beach or in the wilderness of the Angeles National Forrest. Sometimes, we would go on an afternoon drive in the mountains east of Los Angeles. As we got further from the city, I would roll my car window down. The air would be crisp, and I could smell my childhood memories. The whole time we lived in La Crescenta, it felt as if I was close to finding some part of me that had always been missing, like one day I was going to walk around a corner and find the rest of me.

My Love,

You had such a different way of learning and seeing life, but it did not conform to the extremely strict and narrow view of those in authority over you. You very quickly learned to walk in the shadows. You learned that you could be a friend to anyone without ever opening up your heart and being exposed to the possibility of not being loved.

I know what is coming is a bit scary and so uncomfortable, but you need to do your best to forget all of that discomfort and recall in your life the times when you knew who you were.

Go back to the earliest memories you can find. When you were young you had far more confidence. You looked at the world with "big" eyes. Nothing escaped you and you learned from everything. Every moment of your young life, you watched it all unfold in all its wonder. You could literally watch the grass grow. Clouds moved in the sky just to show you that they were actually living things. You could hear the trees. You climbed them further than any child your age should have been able to. You were gifted to see all of the universe in a mud puddle. You were in the perfect environment, living on a mountain in the middle of the forest; until you went to school and someone (who was as big as God in your mind) told you that what you saw was not real.

You must now return to seeing the world with your childhood eyes of wonder. Look for Eternity in everything you see. Listen to the trees again. Let your friends, the clouds, speak to you in loving thoughts that only the two of you know. Go back to the beginning and become you.

Your Eternal Love
(6/28/2022)

Orleans California, winter 1963, Three-years-old with older brother

1964, 4-years-old. With older and younger brother

2

One life changing day

FIRST CONTACT

It was at some point in late1990, when Donna and I finally thought that we should move from La Crescenta to Lancaster, California. Four kids in an 800-square-foot two-bedroom house was just too crowded. A larger home in La Crescenta was way too expensive. Rent was much cheaper the further we got from Los Angeles, enough that we could save several hundred dollars a month. Even with the hour-long commute from Lancaster to Pasadena, life would be better.

We packed up and moved into a fairly new four-bedroom 2800 square foot house that had an above ground pool and enough space for four kids. It was such an upgrade for us. It was a bit like being on vacation every day. And when we sent a naughty kid to their room for fighting with their brothers or sisters, they actually went to a different room. It was possible to have some peace and quiet in the evening. Adult time was a completely new concept to us.

At the time, we were "practicing" Seventh Day Adventists. We had a couple of churches to choose from. On the third week in town, we decided to go to the larger of the two. When we got there, the parking lot was full *and* there were kids everywhere, playing in the parking lot and the big lawn that was next to it.

It was time for services to begin and Donna took the kids to the rooms for their age groups, and I went to the main sanctuary. They were breaking up for study groups and announced that there was a young adult study class. The person leading the class was a large guy, probably six feet five and I estimated that he weighed over 250 pounds. I sat there and listened to him teaching. He had a personality as enormous as he was. There was another man there who wasn't as tall, and I was sure he weighed close to 400 pounds. Between the two of them, there was a lot of laughing.

Afterwards, the class leader Jim came up and asked if I was new to the area or if I was just visiting. I told him that we just moved and were looking for a church family. We started talking, and the other guy introduced himself as Marcos. Just as the conversation between the three of us turned to family, Donna came into the room with our four kids. Our youngest was about two-years-old and in Donna's arms. As I was talking to Jim and Marcos, their wives came in. First Cindy, Jim's wife. Then Marcos's wife, Mari Lynn came in.

What I remember about Mari Lynn was her eyes. They seemed to sear deep into a place that I didn't even know existed. When I saw them, I actually had to look away. I clearly remember not being able to look at her. Even with that, it felt like there was some sort of a magnet trying to draw me back. I was doing my best to live within all the rules that I had been given as a child, even if many of them made no sense.

As we talked, Cindy mentioned that they were planning to get together after church for a potluck at one of their homes but hadn't decided who's. After a quick discussion, Donna and I offered our home because we were more centrally located, and we had the most space. That afternoon we had Jim and Cindy, their two girls, Mari Lynn and Marcos with their two girls, Tom and Rebecca, and Marty and Bobbi over to our new home.

After we ate and the conversations died down, I got my guitar out for some playing and singing in our family room. What I remember most about that day was realizing Mari Lynn was leaning against the wall seated at my knees singing *and* staring straight at me. Her voice was incredibly beautiful. We were singing together on the first afternoon that we had ever met, beginning a life together neither of us could yet imagine.

Mari Lynn February 1995

3

Three Years of Hell and Oblivion

CAMPING AND POOP

The five families grew closer over the next few years. Almost every week after church, we would all be at one house or the other or would go on long weekends camping. Mari Lynn and Marcos and Tom and Rebecca both had motorhomes. We had a large popup tent trailer while Marty and Bobbi had a camper mounted on his Toyota pickup. Jim and Cindy didn't own anything, they would typically spread out with the other families.

One long weekend, we went camping at Bonita Meadows, a remote primitive location on the eastern slopes of the Sierra Nevada mountains. There were zero services there, not even any fresh water. Jim and Cindy, had never been camping and had to buy everything from scratch, including sleeping bags, a tent big enough for the four of them, a camp stove, and even flashlights. They were complete newbies.

We stopped for breakfast a few hours up the road, but when we loaded all the kids back into the cars and motorhomes, Jim was nowhere to be found. I had seen him buy a newspaper and was pretty sure where he was. I went back into the restaurant's restroom and yelled in, "Jim, are you ok?" His quick answer, "Leave me alone, I'm busy." We were back on the road a half hour later. When we got to the campsite, we parked our RVs in whatever flat spots we could find while Jim and Cindy were reading the labels on their tent and sleeping bags to figure out how to use them, but that wasn't their only problem.

Jim almost hadn't come when we told him Bonita Meadows was so remote that toilet facilities were a roll of paper and a shovel. He thought he had this issue well in hand when while shopping for camping gear he found a portable camp toilet. Apparently, he didn't read the label or the weight limit warning.

As soon as it was dark, Jim went and found his camp toilet which consisted of a toilet seat over a disposable plastic bag supported by folding legs. Jim, the toilet, and flashlight went up a nearby hill and disappeared behind some brush. We could see the flashlight shining straight up and all seemed to be going well, until it wasn't. Suddenly there was a primal yell and the flashlight rolled through to our side of the brush. I think what followed was Jim screaming out a list of all the foul language known to man. It took nearly an hour for Jim to clean up and come down the hill. There was a large crash and more language as he threw the mangled camp toilet into the trash dumpster. Jim's misadventure wasn't the end of the trials and tribulations of being new to camping.

The next day, all the kids were out playing in the meadow and stream that ran through it. Six girls from three of the families were having a fantastic time. Everyone but Jim and Cindy had warned their kids about what would happen if they drank the water from the stream. They didn't seem all that worried about it. That night, their little oversight paid off in a huge, explosive way.

After the large campfire began to die down, everyone went to bed, but Jim's girls began not to feel well. Since they were loving parents, Jim and Cindy invited the girls into the double sleeping bag with Mom and Dad. A little after midnight, Jim's voice began to ring out into the otherwise quiet mountain air. This time, Cindy joined him in a chorus of profanity that matched (or even exceeded) the rendition of the previous tragedy. The penalty for not listening to everyone's warning resounded like dynamite because all four of them were in one sleeping bag! Their tent was at least 50 feet from our trailer, but I could smell their problem with our trailer door shut.

Suddenly, there was a knock on our door. It was Cindy with what looked like motor oil smeared all over her hands and smudged across one cheek. Pathetically she asked, "Can you help us? I think we have a problem." If the little girls hadn't been sick, it might actually have been funny, but by now the rest of the adults in the camp were awake and there was nothing amusing about their situation. We all lit lanterns and then pitched in to help Jim and Cindy regain control. Cindy did her best to clean up the little girls, and the rest of us gathered up soiled bedding and clothes, sealed them in garbage bags, and threw them in the bear proof dumpster. The tent was clean enough that Jim and Cindy laid back down in their tent with extra blankets from other families. The ordeal seemed to be over, and we let the two exhausted girls sleep on an extra bed in our trailer. They still smelled so intensely that my eyes were watering on the other side of the trailer.

Even before the group had left home, Mari Lynn had been complaining of a terribly painful toothache. Knowing that Marcos relied on Mari Lynn for everything from cooking and cleaning, to watching their girls, and even maintaining the mechanical systems in their motorhome, we all wondered how Marcos would manage if she wasn't 100 percent.

Mari Lynn seemed to be feeling a little better by Saturday morning and suggested that, rather than each family have separate breakfasts, we should pool our resources. Her girls and Marcos were still sleeping, so the two of us decided that we would use the kitchen in my trailer. We kicked six kids out and before long, Mari Lynn and I were alone cooking breakfast for the entire group. This was one of the first times we found ourselves alone. Just the two of us cooking in the kitchen felt so comfortable, and for a few moments I could feel the universe telling me this was exactly where I should be.

Our five families grew closer and referred to ourselves as "The Friends"; however, the rest of our church began to refer to us as "The Cult". Even though our time together was a great deal of fun, it was getting so we'd be a little frantic if Friday night came and we didn't know what the other four families were doing. In retrospect, our church members' description was probably more accurate.

We became so comfortable with each other that we often displayed our worst behavior. Several times, I watched Marty pay for a soda at a convenience store while he walked out with two or three candy bars in his coat pocket he'd hidden from the cashier. Jim had a quick temper, and on many occasions, I watched him spit on the door handle of a car that parked too close to his, or worse yet, use one of his car keys to dig a deep scratch in a stranger's car for the modest offence of poor parking. Each of us had our own character flaws, and too often allowed them to control our behavior.

Marcos's personality demanded that he be the center of everything, and for the most part, "The Friends" allowed it. If we went to a movie, it was frequently the one that Marcos wanted to see. Doing what he wanted was often easier than dealing with the fallout. If he didn't get his way, he might take his family and go home. Keeping the five families together had become more important than any individual's psychological health.

Often, at one of "The Friends" homes or even at a church potluck (with nearly every church member in attendance), someone would make a comment about how lucky Marcos was to have Mari Lynn working so hard to provide for his family, suggesting that keeping her happy was the only way to maintain their financial status.

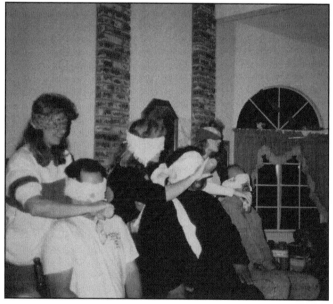

Game night with "The Friends"

Marcos would always respond in the same manner: He would loudly state that everything *she* had was because of him, and if she even considered leaving him, he would "Kill her, my daughters, and then me." If anyone asked if he was serious, he would laugh and say, "Of course, I'm joking." Those of us who knew him best understood the threat to be real, but we had all become so inwardly broken that we outwardly accepted him passing off his ultimatum as a joke. "The Friends" had become "The Cult" our church's members believed it to be.

THE LAKE

"The Friends" made several trips to Lake Havasu, Arizona. There was an RV resort there with a place to moor Mari Lynn and Marcos's and Tom and Rebecca's boats. One trip my two girls wanted to ride with their best friends, Mari Lynn's girls, in their motor home. Marcos said it was okay, but *he* wasn't going to babysit. He wanted Donna to come too. She agreed, but I pointed out that I would have a five-hour drive without any adult conversation. Before I knew it, Mari Lynn was riding shotgun in my minivan. Mari Lynn seemed almost giddy. I didn't really understand why, but I sort of felt the same way. We had five hours to talk about everything or nothing. It just seemed so natural and comfortable, and really fun.

On another trip to the lake, out of the blue, Mari Lynn and Marcos bought a park model trailer that was permanently set up on a lot at the resort. All of us were always amazed at how Mari Lynn was able to juggle their finances. Marcos had always displayed narcissistic traits, and we did our best to allow him to be who he needed to be. How could we possibly sit in judgement? Every one of us was damaged in some way. If what he needed was a facade of success, we were happy to oblige.

Later that weekend, Mari Lynn was riding behind their boat on a new tube they had just bought. She wanted to make sure it was safe for the smaller kids, and as she was riding, Marcos began to drive the boat faster and faster. Then he began to make as tight of turns as possible. We all knew that Mari Lynn had difficulty with her back that could be quite painful. She was now yelling for him to stop. He wasn't listening and actually began to laugh as he accelerated even harder.

Now, everyone in the boat was begging him to stop, but he wouldn't. Finally, I came from behind and reached up, pulled the throttle, and stopped the boat. We pulled the tube to the boat and several of us helped Mari Lynn. She was sobbing and trembling, in obvious pain. As we got her in the boat, Marcos made some joke about her wanting to test the safety of the tube and he claimed he was just doing his part.

When we got back to shore, he hadn't apologized or even acknowledged that she was hurt. I was really angry with him, and so was everybody else. I helped her out of the boat and let her lean on me as she limped to their trailer.

Marcos had made plans to take everyone and the two boats to the London Bridge that had been imported and reassembled in Havasu City. They would be gone for three or four hours. Mari Lynn couldn't even get up to get a drink of water, so, she wasn't going. I was still really pissed at Marcos for being so cruel to a friend of mine that I didn't want to go anywhere with him, so I volunteered to sit with Mari Lynn. My mom who had made the trip with us and had been in the boat, looked at me a little sideways. "Be careful," she said. "I know what I'm doing," I replied. At the time, I didn't think I had a motive other than to be with a friend who needed my help. Again, we were alone for another four hours to talk about anything or nothing. Our relationship was growing without me realizing, giving, or even needing my permission.

Mari Lynn at Lake Havasu, Arizona

By this time, I was beginning to recognize how much better I felt about everything when she was around. I was anticipating her being at every social or church event. If she didn't show up, it felt as if the air had gone stale. I had never felt this way about anyone and didn't understand it. Every time I would recognize the feeling was there, I would push it down as far out of sight as I could.

The group had already recognized how well we worked together, and it became a running joke that Marcos should hire me to help Mari Lynn manage their courier business. They were sure, they said, that the two of us working together would be so successful that he could retire to an island and spend his days sipping umbrella drinks, and that eventually the entire group would be working for Mari Lynn and me.

VOLLEYBALL

"The Friends" were constantly together. We went everywhere and did everything as if we were one big family. We were always at someone's home for tacos or game and movie nights. On Saturday evenings, our church would open the multipurpose room for volleyball. For the first few nights, Mari Lynn and I would always seem to get on the same team. When this happened our team never lost, and we loved it. Soon, the other players began to think that we worked so well together, it wasn't fair. They made a rule that we were not allowed to be teammates.

Marcos and Tim at an Edwards AFB air show

ELVIS

After church one Sabbath, Mari Lynn approached me and asked if I would help her sing for her little sister's wedding. Sherry's favorite love song was "Love Me Tender", and she wanted Mari Lynn to sing it for her. Sherry had agreed to let me accompany her with my guitar and we began rehearsals.

We only had a couple of months, but Mari Lynn was not going to let her little sister down, and for the next two months, we met at Mari Lynn's house. I would sit on the couch and Mari Lynn sat at my feet with her legs crossed in typical Mari Lynn fashion. She had the approved lyrics printed. We were only allowed to sing the first two verses.

The ceremony was in the main sanctuary of a church that was conservative even by SDA standards. Sherry had to get approval from the senior leadership of the church and had convinced them that the two verses now on the coffee table in front of us would be suitable. We would be allowed to sing Sherry's favorite love song–so long as we didn't sound too much like Elvis. We were confident our musical gift to Sherry would go on as planned.

Our rehearsal schedule was surprisingly rigorous for such a simple song. I wondered why we needed so much practice, but I wasn't about to complain about spending extra time with Mari Lynn. We met for two hours, two nights a week until two weeks before the service, then four times each week. We intentionally arranged the song so that Elvis would be the last thing anybody would think about.

Mari Lynn's voice was perfect. I would wait until the chorus and come in with harmony. Our voices were well matched from the very beginning. In order to synchronize the lyrics note-for-note, we focused on each other. I matched Mari Lynn's words and before long we were singing as one voice.

As rehearsals continued, we would often have Marcos or some of our friends in the room listening. "Slow down" he would say, "Don't rush it." Then he looked straight at me and

said something that, to this day, I can't get my head wrapped
around. This man who was possessive and extremely jealous,
who wouldn't let Mari Lynn go play racquetball with a mixed
group of friends looked at me and said with a straight face,
"Look straight into her eyes. Sing it like you're singing the
words to her, about her". When that came out of his mouth,
I saw Mari Lynn blink a couple of times and swallow really hard. For the next several times through the song, both
of our voices seemed pinched, and my fingers were having
trouble finding their marks.

Sherry's day finally arrived. When I found Mari Lynn, she
was very upset. One of the little church ladies had seen the
program and was stirring up quite a fuss about the Elvis song.
She and several of her friends had cornered the senior pastor and was really forcing the issue. If there was going to be
rock'n'roll in the sanctuary, they and their husbands would
leave the service. The real problem for the pastor was that one
of these well-meaning church ladies was *his* wife. When Sherry
came out of her dressing room, just by looking at her tearful
face it was very clear that her favorite love song would not be
part of her perfect forever day. Elvis had left the building.

THE FIGHT

In the late fall or early winter 1993, I was working for the
Antelope Valley Press. M&M Courier, Marcos and Mari

Lynn's business had run into some difficult times and Marcos was barely working while Mari Lynn was working full time at a medical office AND managing their courier service. Marcos just seemed to ignore all of the challenges and basically went on vacation.

One afternoon, I got a call from him. We had a mutual friend who had an old dune buggy that Marcos had offered to buy, and we were going to pick it up. Marcos, Tom, and Jim picked me up in his Suburban pulling a borrowed trailer. When we arrived, we spotted an engine, and two wheels sticking out of three or four feet of overgrown grass under a tree. As we trampled the grass, we found the entire buggy, but all the tires were flat. It looked like it was in extremely poor shape, but Marcos had bought it for a low price, and was certain it could be fully restored and functional for a few hundred dollars.

As we were pulling away, we started talking about where to take it to work on. Marcos's home in Acton did not have a garage and was on a windy hill, so working on it there wasn't really possible. Tom said there was no way in hell he was going to let that old thing in his garage. So we just decided that we would work on it in *my* garage. I hadn't even talked to Donna. That was sort of strike one on our project. We just went to my house and put her prized possession, an Eddi Bauer Aerostar van out of the garage and rolled this old buggy in and started making plans to get it up and running.

It was in pretty bad shape; every piece of rubber was rotted, and all the brake and fuel lines were fouled. The biggest problem of all however, was that the engine wouldn't turn over. After a trip to the buggy and auto parts stores, we started work and disassembled it to the frame. Marcos didn't work on any of the mechanical problems. He spent all his time polishing and cleaning parts and left the actual mechanical work to other people. Once we had it totally taken apart, Marcos wanted to paint it. Donna said he couldn't do it in her garage, because the paint fumes would come into the house and it *might* make her sick. That sort of pissed him off, so he rolled it out onto the lawn and painted the frame right there without *anything* covering the grass. He painted my front lawn blue and thought it was really funny. Donna came out and saw what had happened, she really freaked out about it, and started telling him that he was "stupid" and demanded he explain how he could "do that" to her grass.

When Marcos was young, he was a poor student in school, and his father used to tell him he was "stupid". Donna knew that this insult had extra sting, but she used it anyway. He laughed it off and tried to point out that the grass was already dead. In reality, it wasn't dead except for where he had just spray painted it.

Then, in the most passive aggressive act I've ever seen, Marcos grabbed my electric string trimmer and used it to get rid of all of the blue paint, which meant that he whacked the grass right to the dirt, creating a dune buggy sized bare patch. So now instead of having a blue painted lawn, I had no lawn. He had cut the whole thing to dirt and killed it. Of course, an hour later when Donna saw that, it made the situation much worse.

We eventually got the dune buggy fixed and planned a trip to Dumont Dunes, which is in the California desert near Death Valley about 200 miles from where we lived. All of us traveled in our motorhomes. Tom and Rebecca had quads, Marcos had a quad for his girls and Mari Lynn had her three-wheeler. We all went and had a great time, sort of.

Marcos started getting really weird about his buggy. I felt like I'd earned the right to drive it sometime, but he wasn't happy whenever I'd ask. I don't know if it was the argument that was still festering, or if it was just him being posses-sive of something that he bought. I had worked close to 100 hours getting the mechanics of it functional, cleaned, and safe, and it turned into a classy little buggy.

One late afternoon, I asked Marcos if I could take a drive. Without any explanation, he said, "No!" I wasn't entirely sure why, but when Mari Lynn heard him, she seemed a little pissed off, and said, "I'll take you. We can go and he can't argue. If you want to drive the buggy, I'll take you. It's mine too." All of a sudden, Mari Lynn and I were by ourselves driving off into the sunset. All we could see was sand dunes and sky.

Tim and Marcos in the dune buggy at Dumont Dunes

Mari Lynn and her three-wheeler

Donna and Marcos were still feuding and calling each other names. At group gatherings there were always little snips at each other, and we could tell that tempers were just boiling under the surface. At some point, the insults got really, really personal. Donna had a habit, a nervous twitch; I won't describe it, but Marcos said something about it publicly and ridiculed her for it. She denied it, and again they got into a huge argument. That evening, privately I pointed out that, yes, she did do it and I was suddenly in trouble from her as well and was accused of taking his side.

Marcos was getting angrier and angrier at us. I think he may have known deep down that he was at fault, but there was absolutely no way he would admit it. It was obvious to everyone that Marcos had been the aggressor, and that he initiated the whole situation by spray painting our lawn blue and then killing our grass with a weed whacker.

It got to the point where Marcos became so angry that he stopped talking to *me*. Then their family started not coming to gatherings when we would meet after church or have a meal at a friend's house. For me, that was particularly painful. It wasn't just him that *he* was pulling out of the group, he was removing his family as well. Madison was Joanna's best friend, and Marissa was Jessica's best friend. They weren't allowed to speak to each other anymore, a*nd* (to top the whole situation off) Mari Lynn was no longer allowed to speak to any of us.

It was really difficult, but I thought that I would be the bigger man and called Marcos at home. He wouldn't talk to me; instead he had me talk to Mari Lynn. I asked if there was something I could do, if I could come over, and Marcos and I could just talk about it. We agreed that the next afternoon Marcos would meet me at his home.

When I got to his house, Mari Lynn was the only person there. She said that Marcos wouldn't talk to me, but I could talk on the phone to his brother, Robert. I tried to explain to Robert that even though the argument had become personal, we needed to bury the hatchet, everybody move on, and just let it go. He said Marcos would not do that, and Donna needed to apologize to him publicly because it was her fault. If anything less happened, and if she didn't make this public apology, we would never see his family again except from a distance.

It was obvious that Marcos didn't want to solve the problem. I had done everything I could, but I was unwilling to make a promise to have Donna humiliate herself. I begged to talk directly to Marcos over the phone, but I wasn't allowed to. It really felt like it was destructive to me and my family, so I had to find a way to let it go.

After getting off the phone with Robert, I talked to Mari Lynn for a little while. She told me that this was exactly what he had done before with other people, even family members. She had lived through this with him, and it never ended well unless everyone did what he wanted. They would usually move on to another group of friends. She was really upset as we walked to my car. When we hugged goodbye, I felt like I was never going to see her again.

I think that was the first time I'd *really* hugged Mari Lynn. We had casually touched before, as I helped her in and out of their boat or while playing volleyball at the church. As I look back on it now, those "casual" touches were electric and seemed to create too many questions that had answers I was afraid to hear.

Hugging her felt like I was telling her *goodbye forever*, and not farewell or "see you soon". It was the hardest thing I've ever done in my life. We both just held each other and sobbed. It didn't make any sense to me. Why was I feeling that much emotion? I did not understand it. In the past, I had lost other friendships, but I had never felt this kind of loss before in my life. It literally felt like I was losing part of me.

From that point, (the spring of 1994 to the end of the year) the only time I saw Mari Lynn was from across the church sanctuary. Marcos would sit his family as far away from all of "the Friends" as possible. He would deliberately sit in the line of sight between her and everyone else. Occasionally, a smirk would come across his face. As if he was taunting us, showing everyone what we were missing and that he was in control. She was not allowed to be seen. Their daughters were not allowed to speak to my girls, so my daughters lost their best friends. It was heartbreaking for them. That was pretty much the end of my friendship with Marcos.

THE CHRISTMAS PARTY

There was a Christmas party at one of "The Friends" houses one evening in 1994. I had quit the job at a local newspaper and had begun working for a local businessman who had a small empire of seven different businesses. At 1 a.m. the next morning, I was substituting for one of his newspaper carriers whose route included filling a little over 100 newspaper boxes between Mohave and Bakersfield, CA. I was going to be driving about 300 miles between midnight and 7 a.m. and would have to leave well before the party ended. There was a rumor that Mari Lynn and her family would be there. They had been in self-imposed exile for several months over those very personal arguments between Marcos and Donna. Since she had been taken out of my life, mediocre as my life was, it had begun to completely implode.

In June of that year, as Donna and I were thinking about what we would like to do for July 4th, I thought it would be really fun to have my cousin come up from Los Angeles. When we had lived "down below" he had watched our kids for us nearly every weekend. I was working ten hours a day, and we were living in an 800-square-foot two-bedroom house with four small children. When we needed a break, his help was something we very much needed, and he was really good with the kids.

For the two years or so since we had moved to Lancaster, we just didn't see him that much, and I thought we should at least invite him to our home. When I suggested it, without elaborating, Donna told me she didn't think we should. I pushed her a bit on it, and we got into a sudden unexpected argument. I didn't understand why I shouldn't be allowed to see my cousin. After all, he had been such a huge help for all our time in that little house.

Finally, after several loud hours of arguing, she said, "Fine. I'll tell you, but don't get mad." I didn't see what difference it would make. Nothing she could say at this point could possibly get me any more pissed off. I was so wrong.

After making me sit down, she told me that for the entire two years my cousin was watching our kids, he was molesting our now 12-year-old daughter.

She was right I did get angrier. As a matter of fact, to that point in my life I had never been that enraged about anything, *until* she told me that she had known for over a year-and-a-half! Our daughter had been brave enough to tell her mom about this terrible ordeal. Her mother's response, the person who should have been her protector, was to tell her to keep it secret, that if anyone ever knew it would ruin the family. And for sure, "Do not tell your Daddy!"

My anger, the greatest anger I had ever felt now went beyond rage. All I could think of was getting away from the person in front of me, the mother of my children before I hurt her and lost any ability to repair the unrepairable. I stood up, and without speaking, walked right past her, picked up my car keys and left the house.

I barely got out of the cul-de-sac before I had to pull over and throw up. My head was spinning; I couldn't feel my body. Donna's unforgivable behavior aside, how could *I* have missed this atrocity? I thought about all the times he seemed eager to take *my* kids to his house, about how often it was *my* daughter on his shoulder or on his lap. My sense of failure was overwhelming. I drove around for hours, often having to stop again at the side of the road. I wasn't sure about what might be coming for my cousin. I really didn't care. I did know two things: If it took me the rest of my life, I would make sure my daughter knew that I would do anything, walk through any fire, or tear my own life apart so she would have a chance to be okay and be whole again. I knew my 15-year marriage was over. We might live in the same house; we might even do that for the rest of our lives, but I couldn't imagine any circumstance that I could forgive her. I would never absolve her for being able to look her own daughter in the eyes, a child who had just had the bravery to inform her mother of a two-year long violation AND violate her again by ordering her not to tell me.

When I got home, I went straight to my daughter's room. I held her in my lap, and I told her that I knew. We sat there crying. After about an hour, we got her coat and without even acknowledging my wife sitting on the couch, went out for her favorite fast food.

What I began to realize was that I didn't have the income for the years of therapy this doubly violated child was going to need. It seemed logical that the person responsible should pay for what may be an incredible amount of therapy. At the time, I wasn't even thinking about his punishment or winning justice for my daughter. I only was thinking about a child who, if she was going to have even a small chance of ever having trusting and loving relationships of any kind would need so much help.

It took me a week to get myself prepared to confront my cousin. I called him at his work. As I started explaining why I was calling, he interrupted me. He said that for the past two years, he was anticipating this call. He told me that she was telling the truth and that he had done everything she had said he'd done. I told him my demand wasn't so much for legal justice, but he had better be prepared to pay for multiple years of therapy. He agreed, however, we were both really naive about what would happen next.

In the therapists' intake interview, she stopped us and called our local police department. To my shock, without any real investigation, two weeks later, my cousin was arrested.

The Los Angeles County Assistant District Attorney for Sexual Assaults Against Minors was a young woman with as much fire in her eyes about this atrocity as I had. She gently took my daughter by the hand and interviewed her for four hours. When they came out, she took me aside and told me I had a "very brave daughter", and based on just the notes she had taken, they would be filing at least 15 counts of lewd acts on a minor.

While I was home, I made sure none of my kids saw how this crisis changed me in any way. I was still working incredibly early mornings monitoring newspaper home delivery routes, but as soon as I'd get in my car to drive to work my body would begin to shake uncontrollably. It got to the point where I wasn't safe to drive, even on the early morning empty streets. I had two coworkers, JP and Kim, who were also close friends. They saw the crisis I was in and when I told them, they began doing my job for me. Instead of going to work, I'd go to one of their apartments. I'd curl up on my friends couch and shake uncontrollably while she tried to massage the cramps out of my neck and shoulders. All the while, my other friend was doing all three of our jobs.

My situation was unsustainable, but there was no way I was going to let my daughter see any of the crisis I was experiencing. When I was away from the house though, I was in complete panic attack mode. As a father, I had many ways I could do it, but I really only had one job, to protect my children, and I had failed in the most spectacular way.

I had been raised in a family that really didn't show much emotion. Sure us kids had arguments, even some real knock-down-drag-out-fights, but other than anger, I really never saw any true emotion (either positive or negative) from my parents. I remember, in high school, how shocked I was when my parents actually held hands on vacation once.

I had absolutely no tools to deal with this much emotion flooding my entire body. At the time, I only had two friends, JP and Kim, that I felt I could trust seeing me this way. Donna didn't even know. She had always been unsupportive of any of my personal issues and was now in her own bubble of denial. I felt that exposing myself to the person who had perpetuated this horrifying ordeal would magnify my crisis. I was losing a fight my daughter couldn't afford for me to lose.

When the holidays came, a rumor started going around "The Friends" that Marcos's anger was subsiding and that just maybe we'd all get to see them at a Christmas party. If I could last that long, maybe I could talk to *her*. I just knew deep, deep down that if I could talk to Mari Lynn, I might survive.

We arrived a little late to the Christmas party. They were already singing Christmas carols in the front room, so I got my guitar out and joined the pastor who was already playing.

The only place for me to sit was in a corner across the room from the front door. After a few minutes, the front door burst open and in came Mari Lynn's daughters, followed by their father and Mari Lynn. She looked across the room and we made the briefest eye contact before she was greeted by our hosts and made her way into the kitchen with some food. I could hear her distinct laugh over the singing. I don't know if it was obvious to anyone else, but she seemed worried, like if she had too much fun, Marcos might never let them see this group of friends ever again.

When the singing stopped, I carefully made my way around the house looking for her. There was no way *I* was going to be the reason she was pulled out of my life again. I found her in the kitchen and waited for a brief moment to be alone with her. I said the simplest of things, "I need to talk to you." We didn't touch; we didn't even make any eye contact. I didn't dare because it would have been too much. All my raw emotions of the past few months would have come racing to the surface. She quietly whispered, almost just mouthing her response. "I'll call you," and then I needed to leave.

The holiday season seemed to last forever. I saw Mari Lynn for a moment across our church sanctuary. After the New Year, I was beginning to feel like maybe she had forgotten, or possibly Marcos had retightened the ropes that had taken her from me earlier in the year; but one evening the phone rang. It was Mari Lynn; she could get away the next day for coffee, but I would need to come to her. She was managing the family business but thought she could secretly meet me in the afternoon for an hour or so.

While she needed to keep our meeting secret, I did not. After hanging up the phone, I immediately told Donna that I would be driving to La Cañada the next day to talk to Mari Lynn about our daughter because I needed to confide in someone I trusted.

The next day, I woke up feeling much better. I had a few work-related tasks to get out of the way but was soon driving through the mountains over the Angeles Crest Highway towards a coffee shop where my life was about to change, again, in the most profound way.

FIRST COFFEE

She was already sitting at the counter waiting for me. We each ordered one of the specialty coffees that made this small shop famous. I waited until our drinks arrived before I started, and got her caught up on how my employment had gone downhill since we had last talked. I could see in her eyes that she knew I wasn't there to talk about work. I reluctantly began the story of how miserably I had failed my daughter, of how I was barely holding myself together, of how each and every day that passed, I was sure it would be my last. The only thing that was keeping me alive was knowing what not being there would do to Joanna. I told her how through this nightmare I had become painfully aware that the tools I had as a parent were terribly inadequate. Somehow, I was raising my children in the same way my great-grandparents had been raised over a hundred years ago.

Up to this point, I wasn't able to raise my eyes above my full, (and by now cold) cup of coffee. I felt her compassion before she reached out and gently took my hand. I looked up through my tears and saw that she was crying too. This was the first moment in months that I had the smallest glimmer of hope I might survive this ordeal.

She told me that she felt the same fear for her daughters. Over the next two hours, I heard her tell me of how she was afraid to sleep at night. Marcos was spending hours at night in their living room, and from her bed, she could hear him spinning the cylinder of a revolver. After each spin, there would be a loud click as he pulled the trigger. She was unsure if the gun was loaded, but with each spin she expected the next thing she would hear would be Marcos taking his own life. If this wasn't frightening enough, he had often publicly said that if he ever suspected her of even thinking about leaving their toxic marriage, he would kill her, her daughters, and then himself.

After our server replaced our untouched drinks with fresh hot coffee, we sat in silence as we began to realize that the only way for any of our six children to live safe, happy (and most of all) loving lives was a path that neither of us to this point thought was possible.

I had been raised to believe that there was right and wrong, good and evil, with no gray areas. In 1978, when Donna and I became pregnant with our first child, I believed to the deepest part of my being that the right thing (the only thing) to do was to get married and stay that way the rest of my life. In my beliefs, regardless of my personal happiness, or the well-being of my children, (or even Donna's), the commitment I made as a frightened teenager was permanent. The idea of leaving Donna had always been unthinkable.

I had come to the coffee shop to seek comfort and advice from a friend. Instead, I had found a way to begin to heal generational family sins. As my mind was spinning with the beginning of a completely new belief system, I looked up into eyes that seemed to have the same revelation. Although with the elation and immeasurable joy, there was also a sense of foreboding as we realized the consequences of acting on our newfound understanding.

We knew our church would ostracize us, if not outright throw us out. Many of our family members still believed that divorce was a sin, regardless of abuse or even violence. We also knew "The Friends" could not survive our actions. In an instant, over a cup of coffee, we had thrown a ticking timebomb that, with the force of a nuclear explosion, would alter every part of the lives each of us had known.

If the only consideration had been Mari Lynn's and my happiness, we would have ended our conversation right there, said goodbye, and returned to our friends, spouses, and our church. But the entire point of meeting with Mari Lynn was to ask for her guidance and support after realizing how inadequately I had been taught to be a father. Months before, I had realized how much peril Joanna was in, and *that* realization had opened my eyes to seeing how I was perpetuating a warped view of life and love on all of my children.

Now we saw a course of action, the only way for them to thrive was if we survived and the only way to do that was to do it together. In that brief moment, her two girls and my four children became OUR kids. We were fully committed to showing them a life where love was valued above all else. We completely understood how our church, our families, and everyone important to us would see our actions. We would pay a high price but for them we were gladly willing to pay it.

Mari Lynn was now over three hours late. She had told Marcos that she was going to get her nails done. It was clear there was real danger for her if she couldn't explain why she had been gone so long and her nails looked the same as when she had left the office.

We finally finished our coffee and got up from the counter. I was parked on the sidewalk right outside the door. We talked about needing to meet again VERY soon to figure out how to move forward. Everything had to be done in secret and as fast as possible. If every future action wasn't done in perfect sequence, the timebomb we had just ignited would go off in *our* hands. We kept trying to say goodbye, but the words wouldn't come. There were too many plans to be made. We kept talking and now it was getting dark. The best we could do is exchange pager numbers. (Yes, in 1995 that was still a thing).

At the time, I had no words for what happened as we hugged. In a flash, I had this image race through my mind, and in an instant, I saw thousands of scenes: They were invariably of two people seemingly in every possible situation, facing and conquering all insurmountable human challenges. Somehow, I had been with Mari Lynn before. In spite of all the dangers flooding my mind, I finally felt whole and truly complete, a feeling I had never experienced. I would survive; We would survive, and our children would survive. On January 25, 1995, my life began. Our time had come. We were together and I was home.

Mari Lynn had been aware of our deep spiritual connection for the past three years and living in a sort of limbo, realizing what lay impossibly beyond her reach. For my part, I had been in self-imposed oblivion. Even after hearing our friends constantly joking about Mari Lynn and me getting together, it still took me by surprise. I was the last person to see this coming.

Tim and Mari Lynn on a "Friends" vacation (1993)

Mari Lynn at my house with "The Friends" (1992)

4

Two Pagers, One Plan

Two days after our meeting in La Cañada, my pager went off. It was the signal from Mari Lynn that it was safe to call her. I got to a phone as quickly as I could. She could meet me at noon at a local grocery store. She had exactly one hour. I drove there as quickly as I could and parked in an open area of the parking lot. As soon as I stopped, Mari Lynn pulled up beside me. "Get in." It was all she had to say, and off we charged as fast as we could without being noticed. She reached out, took my hand, and smiled. I could see the wariness in her eyes. We only had a little time and she wanted to make the most of it.

When I thought of writing this book, I made a promise to myself never to write anything that made our kids or grandchildren squeamish. This encounter was the only time that we allowed our passion to be the reason to be together. I think with that promise in mind I'll leave this encounter unwritten.

We never thought of what was occurring as an *"affair"*. I'm sure that most people who find themselves in similar circumstances think of all sorts of reasons or excuses to justify their behavior, but the term didn't seem to fit what we were doing. We had specific goals that involved insuring our children's physical and mental health and if there was any unfaithfulness to us, it would be not being true to ourselves or our children.

Our first concern was the physical safety of Mari Lynn's girls. We knew Marcos would be enraged. He often publicly threatened to kill Mari Lynn, the girls, and himself if she ever left him, and Mari Lynn was terrified for their safety. I had profound concerns about Donna's parenting decisions, but I was never worried about my four children's physical safety, so only four of us would need to temporarily disappear. We decided for the benefit of everyone involved, us, our kids, our friends, and even our spouses, the secret part of our relationship had to be over as quickly as possible.

Mari Lynn and I both had a reputation of being able to manage the shit out of anything. Our friends all knew that if we were working on something together, we could accomplish anything. It was time to put that to the test.

We set a timetable that didn't seem realistic even to us. We planned to be living our new lives together publicly by mid-March 1995, and it was already near the end of January. We decided that if we were going to pull this plan off, we didn't have time to meet solely for a rendezvous like what had just occurred. Within a few minutes, we had a set of pager codes that soon developed into the ability to send several sentences at once. I'm sure we weren't the first people to use this primitive method of texting, but the speed that this language happened even made our heads spin.

My schedule allowed me to come and go from work almost any time I wanted. It was much harder for Mari Lynn to get away. She worked side-by-side with Marcos at their family courier business. However since their business had experienced a downturn a year or so ago, she had returned part time to her old job, managing a medical office. Her friend of ten years was the director of the office and would help cover for her. (This friend knew about me before I knew about me.)

The first problem was how to rent a house. Without any references, any income that we could report, no bank account, and different last names, who would be crazy enough to offer us a lease? Internet advertising for rental property wasn't a "thing" in 1995. Our search for a house not only had to be done secretly, but other than driving around, newspaper ads were our only resource.

We were aware that regardless of our serious and justifiable concerns, California custody laws at the time would likely give Marcos visitation rights if not a temporary split custody order. Donna's transgression, while profound, didn't threaten the children's immediate physical wellbeing, so we were sure there would be a temporary split custody order for my four children. Believing that all six children would eventually be spending time at their other parent's home, we felt we needed to rent a house close enough to Marcos's Acton home and Donna's Palmdale home so that travel back-and-forth would be limited. Lancaster, California seemed perfect. No matter who's home the children were in, Mari Lynn and I would never be more than 20 minutes away.

My pager went off; "911" meant "I need to talk ASAP and it's safe to call back". Mari Lynn had felt compelled to take a detour on her way home from grocery shopping in Lancaster. One street off the main road, she had seen a sign for a home for rent and the landlord had agreed to meet us. We thought we should arrive at the house in the same car. We felt that would look better and would also give us a few moments to get our story straight. Finding this home had come so quickly, we hadn't yet opened a joint bank account, and between us we only had $200 cash. If we were going to rent *this* house, we would need a miracle.

On the way there, we made a single decision that we were determined to make honesty the bedrock of our new life together. We decided to be 100 percent forthright. We felt our separate lives to this point had been based on not even being candid with ourselves. If this was the house we were supposed to have, our new landlord, Mrs. Johnson, would base her decision on the truth of what was about to happen.

When we opened the door to the house, there stood a woman in her late 60's. After a little bit of polite conversation, it was obvious she and Mari Lynn had hit it off. With a simple nod of her head, I knew exactly what Mari Lynn wanted me to do. I made an excuse about wanting to check out the backyard and left the two of them alone in the kitchen. About ten minutes later, Mari Lynn waved me in from a window and we left. When we got in the car, I asked if we got the house.

The woman told Mari Lynn that she had placed the sign in the yard just a half-hour before Mari Lynn had called. She had just lost her husband and was renting their home out and going to live with her daughter. After Mari Lynn told her our story, the lady began to cry. It seems she and her late husband had begun their lives together in a similar way and had been happily married for the past 30 years. Their blended family had become the joy of her life.

Once in the car, Mari Lynn opened her purse and there on top of the $200 were the keys to our new home! Mrs. Johnson would leave a lease for us to sign and wouldn't start charging rent until April—and this was only January! We cried as we drove to my car. Mari Lynn had to race back to the store, but the first miracle had occurred.

Next, we met to open a bank account. Mari Lynn had a rarely used personal account and she put a few hundred dollars from it into *our* new checking account. We needed deposits to get the utilities started for our new home. It was now February. Gas, electric, phone service, and cable TV were all set to start March 1, 1995. By this time, we had less than a month to live in secret.

We were living our lives through pager messages and stolen moments as we would briefly meet in grocery store parking lots where we exchanged notes and letters. We didn't dare spend too much time away from the lives we were trying so desperately to leave.

In late February, I had an out-of-town business event that was a must attend. Several years before, Donna's grandfather had asked me to revive an invention he had gotten patented many years ago. It was a screw in light fixture that, with an internal gear motor, rotated four small incandescent light bulbs. It was designed to be used in retail jewelry display cases. He always felt that if he could solve an overheating problem, it would be a financial success. I had agreed to help and with some changes, created a product that, since it wouldn't start a fire, was headed to UL for testing.

To showcase this new product for the jewelry industry, a friend and I were headed to a Phoenix gem show. He drove a van and set up our display and I flew in a day later. Our display was quite a hit. People could see light dancing from the cubic zirconia facets in our case from 100 yards. Although everyone loved it, no one placed any orders.

While I was walking around the show on a break, I bought two identical pens made from amethyst. One for me and one for Mari Lynn. I thought if we were going to be passing notes like school children, maybe some adult tools would make it seem more grown up.

The moment we got together, something inside of me opened. I'm sure if anyone had asked Mari Lynn, she would have told them that I was a poet in hiding and she had always known it. At the time, I thought she was simply looking at me with eyes that were infatuated. I felt that someday she would come crashing back to earth and see me for the person I really was. I had definitely won the lottery and had found someone that was way out of my league.

I had written a few notes to Mari Lynn, but on the airplane home from Phoenix, I felt compelled to get out my half of our pen set and write something that expressed how much I was missing a part of my life that hadn't yet occurred. What flowed out of me was from a place I didn't know existed. As fast as my hand could move, I wrote to my eternal love. She kept a framed copy of my poem on her desk until the day she passed.

Ever Near

As I sit alone, so far away
I can't seem to find the words
Those feelings strong at last are here
So long have been unstirred

The love I've found is life and breath
And all the world to me
No more in pain, I feel no shame
You're all that I can see

It's not always the one they see
That makes the man a man
Your love for me comes through the air
And lets me know I can

Do all those things I want to do
To fill your heart's desire
In truth, you are my all in all
Your love's my life, my fire

You've shown me now to live my life
The way I should have done
And when I tell the world of you
They'll know you were the one

Who gave me strength and held me close
When life seemed to slip away
I feel you with me ever near
Though now so far away

As we would get chances in rushed phone calls, we began to realize that even though we had been close friends for several years, we had never had a chance to talk about who we were before. We knew each other on such a deep spiritual level, we just didn't know *about* each other. One day, instead of a short note, it was a much thicker envelope. She had written to tell me about the one who held my soul.

Mari Lynn wrote:
"As I sit here trying to work, I can't concentrate. Your presence surrounds me. Your words tell me everything that your thoughts have already said. Through your pen, I can feel your hands touching me, loving me. Nothing you could have given me would I have wanted more. I'm interrupted by your beep. What greater love! I am happy. This is hard to bear to be apart. I need peace. Someday...

You said you knew me, but not about me. What do you want to know? I'm the second child of six. My older sister, Robin, is two years older and perfect. I am not. Even now, I know I will disappoint many people, People that I care about. They'll just have to accept me or not. It was hard being second. Not the oldest, but old enough to have to be responsible for the younger ones.

When I was born, we were living in Joplin, Mo., but the hospital was in Columbus, Ks. So my birth certificate says Ks. We lived in Mo. for four years, then moved here to California. We were here for about three years, and my dad wanted to have *a more rural atmosphere for raising his children. He found a job through <u>The Recorder</u> [an SDA monthly magazine] to run a potato farm in Pine bluffs, Wy. So we moved again. Those memories are some of the best, when I was about seven, riding behind the tractor with my dad planting potatoes. There were irrigation ditches that we would play in. It was beautiful. Cornfields all around. The smell of dirt. There was a barn that wild cats lived in. We always tried to catch them. But my dad wasn't happy. In less than a year we moved to Cheyenne, Wy.*

I don't remember a lot about Cheyenne except that I started first grade there, in a one room school in the back of the Adventist church. We spent only a short time in Cheyenne. Only there was one very, very long blizzard that I remember. It snowed for three days straight. When it stopped, snow was so high around the house that we couldn't get out of it for another day. Then my brothers and sister played around in the snow all the time, while I watched, most of the time, from the window. I would go out for a little bit, but then get so cold I couldn't stand it even to play. I was glad to move.

We moved back to Mo. My dad's mom lived in Joplin, and we lived there for a couple of years. I was in second and third grade there. I had my first crush on a boy named Danny Marcos. The school was bigger, but still grades 1-8 were in one room. I was the only third grader. The school was surrounded by woods. That was neat! One day I fell down at recess and cut my leg on a rock. Allen (an eighth grader) carried me to the teacher's car to take me to the doctors to get stitches. Well, needless to say I now had a crush on Alan. My hero.

My dad took some kind of job that he had to go to England for over a year. I remember him sending us presents on Christmas. By this time, we didn't have much money and had to move in with my grandmother. Her house wasn't big enough for my mom and five kids, so we had this army type tent that was pitched in the backyard. It had all of our stuff in it, and we slept on pallets on the ground. We didn't have to stay there long, but it was an adventure for us kids. I loved being at my grandmother's.

Pause. (You beeped, I called I'm okay. In His time. I'll wait. I love you.)

My dad then went back to California to get another job. Six months later, he told my mom to move back to California. So in the middle of my third grade, we set out to drive cross-country. My mom had five kids, in one car. I remember when we arrived in Sun Valley. It was March and raining; it seemed so gray. My dad had a two bedroom apartment that we lived in for a couple of months. I hated it! I've never lived in an apartment since then.

We then moved to a house right off LA Tuna Canyon in Sun Valley. That was a great house! It was horse property. It had stables in the back and a guest house. But best of all it had an attic. My sister's room was a finished room at the top of the stairs; it even had a bed with drawers built in, but I wanted my own room. So, I would have to walk through the unfinished part of the attic (all open to the rafters), back to a small room that was just drywalled in to make a small room, but it had no window, and that was my room, my hideaway. Adults would have to duck to come into my room.

My mom was pregnant with my youngest sister. My paternal grandmother moved into the guesthouse, I guess to help with all of us kids. I loved to go "visit" my grandmother. She would tell us stories about our ancestors. She was very strict; in church we all had to sit very still. My dad was very strict also. I guess it was hard with so many kids. We knew if we made noise in church, that when we got home, we were going to get a spanking.

When we moved back to California, my mom insisted that we all go to church school. We were members of the Sunland (SDA) Church, so we went to La Crescenta (SDA) School. I started in the middle of my third grade; that was hard. In the middle of the year, in a much bigger school than I'd ever been in, and like I've told you, I've always been very emotional, so all of these things together, I cried a lot at school. Hence, I was called a "crybaby". Well, I got past that, but never liked school. The kids never really seemed to like me!

Pause: ('My endless love is playing. Two hearts that beat is one/ You mean the world to me/ I found in you my endless love/ You will be the only one.')

We lived in the house in Sun Valley for four years. That was the best house. I had a horse that we boarded for one of the church members. I was the one that took care of her. I would feed her and brush her. I would take her out, there were a lot of trails in the hills in Sun Valley. That was great, just being alone and riding. We had every kind of animal at that house, practically. A mule, chickens, ducks, sheep, rabbits, dogs, and cats. I really liked rural living, but I'd live anywhere as long as it was with you.

We then moved to Tujunga. My mom then needed to go to work. She worked nights. At times throughout my childhood, my dad would have bad times (due to work or whatever) and he would start drinking. He would come home drunk, and we would all try to stay out of his way. Usually he would just go to bed. This was in 1972. Between here and 1975, I can't write about it. I'll tell you though, later.

In 1975, we were living in Sunland going to the same church. I was graduating out of eighth grade. I always felt older than I was. I was really close to my older sister and even though she was two years older, everyone thought I was the older one. She is littler than I am. Because of my size, I went into the(church) youth class when I was young. They were a fun bunch of kids. We had a very active youth group at the time. I was always looking for someone like me. Well, I finally got Marcos to notice me. We dated (much to my parent's dislike) on and off all throughout my high school years. Then at the end of my junior year, I only needed a few credits to have enough to graduate, but the school wouldn't let me graduate early. I would have to do a whole senior year. I never really liked the kids in my class. My friends throughout high school were mostly upperclassmen, so I decided to take the GED test. I passed and was done with high school in 1978. Marcos and I got married in April 1979. I was finally on my own. I had a job,

Mari Lynn at Glendale Adventist Academy (1977)

a house, and a husband. Wasn't that what everyone wanted me to do?

That's my life in a nutshell. Some good, some bad, but I want the rest to be happy. It maybe hard, but happy. Our children need to know what's really important. How do we show them what love is if we keep it hidden. One day, we must tell the world. For our good and theirs. Your words comfort me; I read them over and over and am amazed. Where has this person been? A poet, a lover, a friend and so much more. You could do anything you want to. The future is ours

After I read it, Holy Crap! I sat there stunned. While the precise details were a *bit* different, it sounded like we were raised nearly identically, both second children that somehow had to become the responsible ones. We had both attended single room SDA schools. We had both lived in California when we were young and had moved several times including to the mid-west. Obviously, we were both raised as Seventh Day Adventists. My next note was simply, "About your letter, Yeah, me too."

Later that week, I gave her another little poem that came from nowhere.

This Pen

If this pen is all I ever have
To show that I love you
I'll write my thoughts, my feelings deep
And somehow make it through

And if life be lost, our love cut short
My time come to an end
With my last ounce of strength, I'll write
I love you with this pen

But if given time by God above
I'm sure I'll find a way
To spend the moments in your arms
Each and every day

Our schedule was rushed. We were living two lives and getting almost no sleep. There was one Sunday when our secret and public lives intersected. The motorhome that Mari Lynn and Marcos owned needed a little work and they had asked "The Friends" to come over for a work party and barbeque. As crazy as it sounds Marcos asked us, Mari Lynn AND me, to work on the roof vents. That day, we had four hours of being alone in a crowd of unsuspecting friends. Every moment together felt like the air was filled with static electricity, a sensation that continues to this day.

We were terrified for Mari Lynn and her girls. Marcos had always publicly said he would kill Mari Lynn, his girls, and himself if he suspected she was considering leaving him. When anyone would challenge his threats, he would pass it off as a joke. Now his threats seemed to have a more serious quality. We thought it was just us being oversensitive, except other friends noticed and commented on the change as well.

The time had come for Mari Lynn and me to bring our relationship into the sunlight. We had set a date. We wanted to make sure that when we pulled the trigger, everyone knew we were serious and that there would be no going back. We were extremely concerned that our friends and our church would do everything they could to "fix" us. We had to make it stick. Mari Lynn had found an attorney and had started the process of filing for divorce. We felt that while it might not happen, there was still a very real chance that Marcos would act with violence. Our leaving had to happen in not just one day, but in a few hours. All parts of our plan had to go flawlessly and in perfect sequence.

March 14th came; it was the night before we were going to disappear. Because we felt there was a credible threat of physical harm to her two girls, they would have to disappear with us. We didn't believe there were threats of physical harm to my four kids so they would remain with their mom, my soon to be ex. Still, I needed to make sure they would be emotionally okay for the next week or so. We hoped that if enough time passed, Marcos's anger might subside a bit. Our decision to take Mari Lynn's daughters with us created a terrifying but delicate balance. We had to protect them, but Mari Lynn's attorney warned us, "If they are missing too long, it would feed an untrue narrative of child abduction that Marcos could exploit to gain full custody."

TICK TOCK

At 9 p.m. March 14, 1995, the first tick of our clock struck. We each called a friend to explain what was going to happen the next morning and most of all WHY. I called Jim and asked him to meet me at a coffee shop. As we sat down, he said, "I know this is serious, you've never called this late just to talk." I started to tell him, and he began to cry. As tears filled his eyes he said, "I knew this was coming. You don't have to explain. This is going to destroy our group of friends, but it's by far the best thing for the two of you AND by far the best thing long term for your six kids." I asked him if for the next week or so he would look in on Donna and my kids, and that I would be forever in his debt. **"Just make sure they know I'm coming back very soon."** Mari Lynn called Rebecca, a friend close enough that Mari Lynn had often confided in regarding Marcos and their toxic marriage. Their conversation went almost the same way, except Rebecca offered to help with the next part of our clockwork.

The next morning, I left my house at exactly 7:30 a.m. My job was to pick up the reserved U-Haul truck and meet Mari Lynn at her Acton home. Mari Lynn was dropping her two girls at school in La Crescenta just like every other Wednesday and depending on traffic, she should be back home by 8:30 as well. Rebecca and my work friend, JP who had done my job for me while I was in crisis would also meet us in Acton.

As soon as Mari Lynn arrived with house keys, our first task was to locate and hide all seven guns that Marcos owned. He'd have to find another way to kill us. We were not going to take any of them with us because that just sounded like we would be asking for armed war if we were ever confronted. As soon as that was done, we began loading the moving van with Mari Lynn's personal things and some of the furniture. They had two refrigerators and two couches, so one of each went with us. Mari Lynn felt it would be inconceivable that her girls would live with a man who had publicly threatened them and had been playing with his revolver every night for the past several months. So, it went without saying that most of their bedroom furniture and clothes were also loaded in the van.

Anyone who has ever moved knows how time-consuming packing is and how many small tasks there can be. We couldn't move a refrigerator full of groceries and the girls' beds needed disassembled just to get them out of the bedrooms. The four of us filled a 16-foot box van and drove away in less than two hours.

Our two friends and I took the van packed to the hilt with her things to our new house. This was the first time anyone (except Mari Lynn and I) knew that this house even existed. Since I had rented the truck for only a half day, it needed to be returned by noon. We had an hour to unload it.

Mari Lynn had her own schedule to keep. She had to go to her credit union in Glendale to cash out her 401k. It had been funded through her job at the medical office and the $10,000 would pay the bills until she could find a job. We both knew that in California that money was jointly held by her, and Marcos and she had no intention of keeping his share. Mari Lynn was ethical to a fault. But for now, until things got sorted out, it was a way for her to make sure her daughters had food, shelter, and most of all safety.

As soon as she was done at the bank, she was going to pick her daughters up early from school and meet me at our new home by 1:30 p.m. She would do her best to explain what was going on as she drove.

As more chess pieces were flying off the board, timing became more and more critical. As soon as I dropped the U-Haul off, I needed to take my little Mazda truck back to my house and get my clothes. My four kids were off from school so they would be home. I had about a half an hour to try to explain to MY kids what was happening; that I was leaving their mother and I had very good reasons but not enough time to explain my actions to them. They had to believe me, that no matter how it felt, I WAS NOT LEAVING THEM. I would be back as soon as it was safe.

Of course, and justifiably so, Donna was incredibly angry. She threw the alarm clock from my side of the bed at me as well as anything else she could pick up, she threatened me; then she said something that did actually scare the shit out of me: "Does Marcos know? I'm calling him right now!" I had to go, and now! If he found out too soon, we would all be in terrible trouble.

I got to the new house and pulled my truck into the garage about five minutes before Mari Lynn and her girls got there. Our friends, JP and Rebecca, were just leaving as Jim came walking up the drive towards the door. Somehow, he had found us. Had he changed his mind? Or worse yet, did

Marcos know where we were and had he found the guns? The answer was no, at least Jim didn't think so. He was coming to tell Mari Lynn goodbye. The lines were being drawn and we were losing all our friends. Rebecca was crying, and she hugged us as if it was the last time we would ever see her. Unfortunately that *was* the last time she spoke to us as friends.

At 2 p.m., now alone with the girls, we packed what we could, got into Mari Lynn's car, and drove towards the Los Angeles rush hour traffic. At 3 p.m., Marcos was served with divorce papers. It was official. No more secrets. But we had kicked a hornet's nest that would continue to sting us until the day she died.

After we had been driving in complete silence for about an hour, I had a horrifying thought. I looked at her and began to ask her a question. Before I got half a word out, she said," I turned it off and changed the password last night." Because of some quirk in their personal finances, her name was the only one on the car's registration. The night before, she had contacted the auto theft tracking system and had disabled it.

PART 2
(During)

5

21 Years of Bliss, Sort of…

THE ESCAPE

As we drove through LA rush hour traffic, we kept looking over our shoulders. We were scanning the traffic for cars that seemed familiar and we were looking back as well. Everything we held dear was at risk. Terribly frightened, we were in totally unfamiliar territory.

Mari Lynn's best friend in the world, Mabel, someone who knew about me before I did, about how Mari Lynn, from the first day she and I had met, had believed this day would arrive, had a newly acquired vacation home in Pismo Beach, CA., that no one other than her husband knew about. It would be safe for us there—if we could ever get there. There were several accidents on the already crowded Los Angeles freeways. We still had about 130 miles to go, but the girls needed to stop and we decided to get gas too. Mari Lynn had a gas credit card that was in her name. It was declined;

Marcos had reported it stolen and the station attendant kept it. We had the $10,000, but had hoped not to need it so soon. Besides, our location, at least where we stopped for gas, was no longer secret. We *could* have stopped in Moorpark where we were, and stayed with Mari Lynn's mom, or turned southeast towards Santa Monica, south towards Malibu, or even gone north towards Sacramento and Mari Lynn's sister. We had stopped at exactly the right place. Marcos knew where we were but could not possibly know where we were going. Was it a miracle or dumb luck that we stopped exactly where we did? At this point, we didn't care and were not keeping score.

Traffic continued to be terrible. It was after 8 p.m., and the girls hadn't eaten since lunch, but at the next exit was a freeway-side Denny's. Everyone's nerves were on edge. The girls had no concept of the terrified worry that Mari Lynn was carrying. They had no idea of the fear she had lived with the past several years. Mari Lynn had been successful in shielding them from their father's worst behavior, they thought they had lived in a well-adjusted and happy family. What was happening to them made no sense at all. When we finally made it to the condo, it was late enough so that Mari Lynn was able to put the girls to bed, but there was still work for us to do.

One of Mari Lynn's best friends since high school was also married to Marcos's younger brother, Alex. She was our first phone call. Mari Lynn and Dani spoke for a few minutes.

Then Mari Lynn handed me the phone and said, "*He* wants to talk to you." I was about to talk to Marcos's brother, and I didn't know what to expect. "That SOB had it coming! What took you guys this fucking long?" We had allies in the strangest place, her soon-to-be ex-brother and sister-in-law.

The news from them was a little unexpected. Most of our church was now at Mari Lynn's house. The pastor, our friends, including Rebecca (who had just earlier helped us) as well as many people that had recently referred to our group of friends as "a cult", were consoling a man who they had all heard publicly threaten to kill his family. While what had just happened to him must have been overwhelming, anyone who knew him was aware that the only emotion he was feeling was fury that his most prized possession, his white, blonde wife, had publicly embarrassed him.

I had been his friend for the past several years. Mari Lynn had been married to him since 1979. We both knew his narcissistic personality would go through various stages of rage and playing the victim; but the quickness that he had gathered an army to his side was beyond our imagination. The battle lines were drawn. While we had Mabel and Dani and Alex, he had everyone else.

The Saturday before we left, Mari Lynn had quietly told her mom and siblings about what she was going to do. She had gone to Moorpark to see her newborn niece, a daytrip Marcos did not take. While her family had never approved of her interracial marriage to Marcos, they really disapproved of her leaving her marriage and getting a divorce. In God's eyes, marriage was sacred and forever, even if it was abusive and occasionally violent. They all said that even though they disapproved, they would keep her secret until she was safely out of town.

Mari Lynn called her younger brother to tell him she was safe. He told her that Marcos had already called and told him that she had kidnapped his girls and that he had already called the police. He strongly told us, "DO NOT tell anyone where you are!" He also added that he was *very* afraid for our safety.

Next, I called my mom. She said that she was expecting my call. She had already heard from Donna who was at Marcos's house with my kids and the rest of our friends as well as everyone from church. While he was crying in front of everyone, Donna had overheard his conversation with one of his brothers, the commander of the Burbank Police Department's helicopter division, telling him that he wanted us found. His brother wasn't to tell anyone, "Just find them! I'll deal with it." My mom was cautiously supportive of our decision to leave, but was extremely afraid for us.

So now it was my mom and her partner, Dani and Alex, Mari Lynn's family (sort of), and Mabel against everyone else. This handful of people would be our only support for a long, long time. Needless to say, it was a deeply emotional time for me. I began to realize that while the two girls were safe, my kids were now with someone who *really* hated me, and they were experiencing the circus that Marcos and Donna had created with the help of our "Friends" and church.

I began to realize that I had left my children with the person who had made the decision to keep the secret that had ended our marriage, someone I no longer trusted to have credible judgement. Now, she also really hated me and I believed that I would never see any of my kids again. The panic attacks that I had experienced on my friend's couch were back. The longer I left James, Joanna, Josh, and Jessica in that toxic atmosphere, the more likely they would believe the story already spun, that I had been seduced by Mari Lynn and we were using Marcos's girls as weapons. There was a difference in fighting the panic attacks this time. The person who had been able to comfort me with a single touch in that coffee shop was standing next to me. We stayed at Pismo for about a week. Mari Lynn's attorney thought that was about the limit before our actions would begin to support Marcos's claim that we had abducted his girls against their will. We needed to get them back anyway, especially since they had missed a week of school.

REALITY

By the time we returned home, Marcos had hired an attorney of his own. I'm not sure where he found this man. He must have put out an ad for the angriest, most unethical person in all of Los Angeles. Mari Lynn's lawyer was a widowed, Christian grandmother who accepted our case as her last before she retired. The asymmetry of the coming court battle was staggering. Mari Lynn refused to lie. Every document, every single argument was the absolute truth as we understood it. Marcos's lawyer wasn't above anything. He would exploit every dirty trick available to him. In an emergency custody judgement, Marcos would have the girls every other weekend. They would now be exposed to the circus of support he had gathered.

Of course, the girls were thrilled to see their Papi. But some disturbing trends began almost immediately. Marcos refused to talk to Mari Lynn. Every communication from him was by fax. When the girls went back and forth from his home, it looked more like a prisoner exchange in the DMZ. Marcos would drive, and as soon as the car stopped, his brother Robert would get out and open the back door for the girls. He would escort them halfway up our sidewalk, then the girls would walk, ever so slowly, towards the front door and stop before they went in. On nearly every return, one of them would recite whatever communication their dad wanted Mari Lynn to hear. Most times, it included some pretty hateful things in language it was obvious they didn't understand. There was one occasion that Marissa looked straight at me and said," You're a jiggle load!" In the moment it was both hilarious and terrifying. "I'm a what? Where did you hear that?" "My grandma. "She says you're a very bad man that wants to steal us and I need to hate you forever."

Mari Lynn's and Marcos' relationship had ceased to be physically abusive many years earlier; it no longer needed to be. Over their years of dating, he would often be rough, hitting her, and a couple of times pinning her by the neck with her feet off the ground. She had left him several times, but each time he would become despondent and threaten to end his own life. For reasons she could not explain, she would always makeup and go back to him. Those were decisions that she was now beyond regret. Since that time of physical abuse, he was able to control her by a simple word or glance that reminded her of who was in charge.

Now that she was forced to confront him, she spent the night before the coming custody hearing throwing up, something she never did. We were sitting on a bench in a grand marble hallway and Mari Lynn was shaking uncontrollably, with tears streaming down her face. Her soon-to-be ex-husband was entering the courtroom she had just left. As he passed, he'd given her a look, a look he had always used to tell her she could never win.

This hearing was their first child custody arbitration. The process was for each to have an individual interview before sitting together with the arbitrator. There could be no law-yers present. This occasion would be the first time they'd even spoken since she'd left him two months before, let alone appear in the same room together.

Their fight was becoming intense. Mari Lynn was not just afraid she could lose her daughters; she was also afraid for all three of their lives. He had done everything he could to make sure that Mari Lynn was terrified, and would stay that way. There could be no doubt he would do anything to win. It wasn't just that he wanted his children, most importantly, he wanted to make sure Mari Lynn lost them.

She knew him and his tactics. He would do or say anything to get what he wanted. She felt trapped. At the time, the stakes could not possibly be higher. The questions were: Would *she* bend to the pressure and do whatever it took (stoop to his level and lie) to keep her daughters, or would she risk everything by telling the absolute truth.

Mari Lynn was sitting on the wooden bench, and shaking with fear. Her makeup began to run down her cheeks, so she excused herself to go to the ladies' room to wash her face. When she returned, I handed her a folded piece of paper with what I'd written while she was gone.

You Have Already Won

"It's not whether you win or lose, it's how you play the game.[1]" A great coach, I think it was Vince Lombardi said, "Winning is not everything it's the only thing.[2]" I believe this statement is true, but what is it to win? Can there be any victory if the battle is not won with truth? Are we really in the fight to win if we do not embrace what we know to be right in our hearts?

The pursuit of truth and right is the only field where the game of life is played. If we do not seek to self-adjust to what we know is right at every opportunity, then we've removed ourselves from competition. We have forfeited the match.

There are a few sports that have only ourselves as the competitor. I believe this is also true in life. At every opportunity, if we do not seek out the often-painful process of self-reflection, if we do not self-adjust, we're fooling ourselves. We shadowbox. No one will get hurt if blows of self-truth are only seen in a mirror. They must connect; they must be real. We must learn to take that punch in the game of life. The only way to play is also the only way to win. Live life in truth and you have won. With truth you win."

No one can beat you, no one but yourself.

[1] Grantland Rice, Sportswriter

[2] Vince Lombardi, First Day of Training Camp, 1959

It was pretty simple, if she got custody by lying, we would be no better than those who were lying to her girls and would be continuing to live the example we were trying NOT to show our kids. We had many sleepless nights so far and there would be many, many more; but we had already decided there wouldn't be a moment that our consciences would be responsible for a single one.

Looking back, I'm sure we made mistakes. We certainly weren't perfect parents, and there are definitely things we regretted, but to this day, if given the same information we had at that time, we would do *nothing* differently.

REALITY PART DEUX

The outcome of the arbitration hearing was devastating for Mari Lynn. There would be 50/50 temporary custody. The arbitrator felt that Mari Lynn's abuse concerns could be addressed if both girls would go to weekly therapy sessions. They would be spending half of their time with their father.

Regardless of the court order, Marcos refused to take the girls to therapy with the excuse that they didn't like it. He had always said that "only weak people go to therapy", so we weren't surprised. What did surprise us was that we couldn't get the court to do anything about it.

Even though it was difficult, we had made it not just a decision, but a priority, to never let any of the six kids hear us talk poorly in any way about their other parents. Our soon-to-be exes had the exact opposite philosophy. Mari Lynn's oldest daughter became more-and-more withdrawn. The youngest was parroting every hateful phrase imaginable.

My four kids seemed to be adjusting a little better. Their mother wasn't quite as vocal about her hatred. However, one afternoon a month or two into our custody issues, I went over to pick them up and a man answered the door. From the doorway he yelled back into the house, "Honey, your ex is here to pick up *our* kids." From the back of the house, I heard Donna yell back, "Kids, get your coats. Make sure you hug "Daddy Sean before you leave." That whole scenario was unexpected. Just weeks in, someone else was living with my children, and while they seemed to adjust quickly to the idea of a stepfather, I did not. After Donna's betrayal of keeping our daughter's molestation secret, I could not trust, or even understand, how she made major life decisions. Mari Lynn and I weren't naïve and expected that at some point all of our children would have stepparents. We just didn't anticipate a complication as large as an adult we did not know having influence in our childrens lives this soon.

A JOB

It had been almost 15 years since Mari Lynn had had to look for a job. Before she left high school she had worked, first for The Voice of Prophecy, an SDA institution, then she was recommended by a church member to start at Glendale Adventist Medical Center. She worked in medical billing and eventually transferred to run the front office of the hospital's family practice residency program. There she met and became friends with Mabel. Around 1990, Mari Lynn and Marcos Sanchez started M&M Courier business serving the TV and film industries in the Burbank area. Even though she was working full time with the medical office, it was no secret that she was the driving force behind the family business. After a couple of years, the business was successful enough that she was able to stop working at the medical office full-time. Just before she and I made our escape, she was back working part-time at the medical office. Of course, when we left, she would no longer be able to work with M&M Courier. She really felt she had left Marcos with a reasonably successful business that could support her ex-husband's lifestyle. To her, it was extremely important that both of her girls' parents be financially stable.

For the first time in her life, Mari Lynn would need to create a resume and look for employment. She was quite confident about her abilities. She had run the front of a medical office that supported about 25 physicians and had excellent references from there. She had started and operated a successful family business, but references from there would be nonexistent (or worse). Unfortunately, every employment opportunity that would pay her a reasonable salary required a college degree. Mari Lynn didn't even have a high school diploma. She felt seriously undereducated in a workforce where, just months earlier she was telling doctors what to do. In reality, the most significant problem we had was her self-esteem. For over 20 years, she had heard Marcos's voice in her head telling her that she wasn't good enough; that the only reason she had anything was him. After all that time, she believed him.

After a week or so of encouragement from me, we started sending off her resumes. She went on a couple of interviews, but it always came down to her education. Finally, one evening the phone rang, and the voice on the other end asked if she would be able to be in downtown LA the next day around noon. When she got home the next afternoon, she seemed to float into the house. She was in tears as she told me that she was starting work Monday as the executive assistant to the owner of a high-end printing company. Her starting salary was $20k more than she had ever made in her life. Over the next few years, Mari Lynn became the owner's right hand—another miracle.

THERAPY AND PARENTING?

We were juggling two divorces with custody fights over six kids and two full time jobs. It was about this time that my cousin's trial was beginning as well. Donna had already decided that going to any of these proceedings was too much for her. My daughter was sharing time between households. Mari Lynn and I had gone to every single hearing. If Joanna wasn't needed in court, she went to school or stayed with her mom. The few times she was required to be present, Mari Lynn and I took her.

Because Joanna was the victim of a violent crime, Los Angeles County provided a $10,000 grant for therapy for her and her parents. At the recommendation of Dani and Alex, we got an appointment with the family therapist they were seeing. Her schedule was full, and she wasn't accepting new patients, but after hearing Joanna's story (and with Dani and Alex's reference) she agreed to begin work with Joanna and her parents. Somehow, we had backed into one of the preeminent childhood trauma and family therapists on the West Coast. Not only did she provide much needed therapy for Joanna, but she helped us understand the best way forward with our blended family and all the challenges we faced from tag teaming exes. Over the next year and with a huge amount of study, Mari Lynn and I received a certificate as Master Parents.

Mari Lynn's custody situation was approaching time for a permanent decision. The process required a court appointed psychological evaluator to interview both Marcos and Mari Lynn and their two daughters. There would be interviews for any family member as well, including my four kids and me. Interestingly enough, Marcos's new girlfriend would be interviewed too.

Our lawyer got a copy of the report two days before the hearing for us to review. When we read it, we were devastated. The judge hearing our case was equally shocked. He said in his 20 years in family law he had never seen a report like this one. There, in black and white, the evaluator said that due to the older child having lived in Marcos's home and having been allowed to refuse therapy, that she was completely lost to the hateful environment. She was irreparably brainwashed. He told the court that if it acted immediately the younger daughter could be saved IF she was removed from his home.

Two weeks later we received the news. The final custody order was still 50/50. The judge had ignored the evaluator's plea.

$100,000 MISSING?

Since Marcos retained the courier business, the court ordered him to continue making payments on the cars, boat, motorhome, and mortgage on their home until the divorce reached a property settlement. He was in possession of everything except the car Mari Lynn was using. It wasn't clear if it was his lawyer or if he just couldn't stand paying for anything she was using, but he stopped making car payments.

Marcos hadn't changed any passwords on any of their financial accounts. So, Mari Lynn was able to monitor the payments he was making. She could have cleaned out all of their joint accounts, but instead, she had a front row seat as he systematically destroyed everything they had built.

We couldn't afford the car payment yet, so we requested and were granted an emergency hearing. When the court asked him why he wasn't making the car payments, it became clear what he was trying to do. In open court, his attorney accused Mari Lynn of embezzling $100k from the family business and because of that, the business was failing. "They had forensic accountants pouring over the books and would return with proof soon." This accusation was beyond ridiculous. The business NEVER had that much money. Marcos always wanted to spend everything the business made, and Mari Lynn was a genius at the financial shell game it took to keep up their lifestyle. Two things were completely clear: First, just as everyone suspected, Marcos had no idea how to read a financial ledger or run a business for that matter. Second, he was willing to lose everything if it meant Mari Lynn wouldn't keep even the smallest part of the life she had helped build for them.

We could see the humiliation coming. We even stopped keeping any personal items in the car, but where it happened could not have been more embarrassing. In the private parking lot and in front of the woman who had hired her two weeks prior, as well as several co-workers, Mari Lynn's car was repossessed. Mari Lynn was mortified, but Jackie, her employer, was already a good friend. She let Mari Lynn use her brand-new BMW to pick me up from work. The next morning, we returned Jackie's BMW, and began using my 15-year-old compact Mazda pickup for both of our daily commutes. Using one car meant that one of us would get to work a half hour early, and due to Los Angeles evening traffic, would wait to be picked up for over an hour. Our complicated travel to and from work was solved two months later when Mari Lynn's brother bought a car at auction and then sold it to us in monthly installments that we could afford. Mari Lynn fell in love with her "new" sportscar, a red 1987 Nissan Maxima.

Another result of Marcos claiming that the business was losing money was that his income was officially set at minimum wage. The court determined based on the current incomes (and even though the custody was 50/50) that Mari Lynn owed around $1600 a month in child support as well as the cost for Madison's private school tuition. Asymmetry!

NEW JOB

I was still employed for a local businessman in Lancaster and working 60 or more hours a week at near minimum wage. My soon-to-be ex's household expenses hadn't changed. So, to support her and my kids, I would sign my paycheck over to her. Working so hard for so little with hours that were at inconsistent times of the day wasn't sustainable.

I began to look for a better job. I interviewed and was hired at a national company that leased and rented test and measurement equipment as well as computers to businesses. In my interview, I was asked why I was trying to get a job that was obviously below my qualifications. I explained my situation and told them I just wanted my foot in the door. I was willing to take a chance if they were. I was hired as a laborer in the receiving department. It was a solid 9-to-5 job with what seemed to be reasonable benefits, unloading UPS, FedEx, and other carriers all day. Within 2 months, I was named lead of our five-man crew, and 6 months later, promoted to the position of Administrative Supervisor for the Western Distribution Center (WDC), the facility where I worked. I was responsible for the team that ordered service and repair parts. My staff and I tracked up to 6,000 concurrent repairs.

6

January 6, 1996

The end of 1995 was approaching. Though the property and child custody issues were nowhere near resolved, Mari Lynn's divorce was final. For the first time since 1979, she was not Mari Lynn Sanchez. My divorce hadn't been as overtly contentious, but it was taking more time. We had already set a date for our wedding, January 6, 1996. Six was Mari Lynn's favorite number but she was not going to wait until 6/6/96.

We had already booked a wedding chapel in Big Bear, a winter resort in the mountains, a little east of Los Angeles. Winter was their peak time, so even though my divorce wasn't complete, we *had* to book early. The days were counting down. At every opportunity, Donna was reminding me that if it didn't come through, if our divorce wasn't final, Mari Lynn and I wouldn't be able to have our day. Well, with ten days to spare, it came through. We would be married as planned.

We celebrated Christmas Eve with her mom and family and spent Christmas morning with my mom. By this time, Madison had begun refusing to come to our home. Through notes from her, and letters from Robert, Marcos's brother, Madison had told Mari Lynn how much she hated her and that she never wanted to live with or even visit her mother. She demanded that her mom return her stuff to her dad's house. No matter what decisions Mari Lynn made, Madison's anger was growing. More-and-more she was parroting the exact words of her father. We made the painful decision to honor her wish and return her things.

Now, we were about to get married and one of the reasons for us to be together was not going to be there. It broke our hearts, but the only way for us was forward. The night before our wedding, we rented one of the larger cabins on the chapel property where our about-to-be officially blended family would sleep.

The next day, we were joined by our moms, Mari Lynn's brothers, one sister and their families, Dani and Alex, their three kids, in addition to my grandpa and his wife. We had a chance to sing a song to each other that several years before, we had rehearsed over and over. Even though Mari Lynn's and my voices wouldn't cooperate, and my fingers seemed to have completely forgotten how to play a guitar, there wasn't a dry eye in the chapel. Elvis was back in the building.

Of course, we had written our vows and our voices trembled as we read them. They were important, but everyone there already knew how committed we were to each other. What they did not know was the most important thing that happened that day was our public promise to our children. Even though there were only five kids there, the vow was, and always will be to all six.

For the Children

In hope, in dreams, In truth and love
Our greatest wish, Our prayer above
Is that you'll know, Deep in your heart
That on this Day, Our lives will start
To share, to grow, To learn to see,
To be the ones we're meant to be

In pride we see you, and in love we know
That if we let you, You will grow
For on this day, Before God above
We pledge to you unconditional love

Our lives together, Each one so dear,
If you listen, You will hear
In words and deeds, In every way,
We love you, OUR children. And will always

We had made it this far: In less than a year, we had gone from a quiet meeting in a La Cañada coffee shop where the universe opened up, to a snowy wedding chapel in the mountains where we publicly declared our mission of love.

My Dearest Love,

I was sitting with you as you watched the video of our wedding. That was such a fantastic day! What we read for our children still chokes me up a bit. I don't think anyone there caught how important that moment was for us. It was the entire point of us being together.

Of course, I know how it made us feel to be together. It was, at one instant, an end and also a beginning. It was a recognition of the end of our searching for one another. It also marked the beginning of a life of love that all earthly souls are longing for. Yes, I remember all the stress there was around getting ready for that day. We had actually booked the hotel and wedding chapel before your divorce was final. That had happened only a few days before and could have made a real mess of things if it hadn't come through when it did. Our wedding was only nine months after we moved in together and less than a year since our coffee in La Canada that beautiful January day.

What a crazy but amazing year that was, so much real life was shoved in those 12 months. That year took a tremendous amount of very hard work. Think about it for a minute: We both had divorces. We were forced into bankruptcies that were completely avoidable. And of course, there was your cousin's trial. Then remember that I was unemployed, since I was unable to work for the courier business that Marcos and I had started. Mixed in were our therapy sessions for your daughter that turned into family therapy that turned into parenting classes that gained us a certificate as Master Parents. In the first few weeks (1/25/95 to 3/15/95), we had our coffee, filed for two divorces, convinced a very nice lady to rent us a home, set up utilities from phone and electric to cable TV. The pace of that first year was incredible, but it was also the most wonderful and beautiful year I had ever had.

Just like you, the emptiness that I had felt my entire life had been filled. I had been searching for something. Because of how I was raised I thought the emptiness was supposed to be answered with religion. As you, I tried really hard to fit that religious square peg into the round hole I experienced in my life. When we met in that church classroom, I had a sudden realization that I just encountered a glimpse of exactly what was missing from my life. If you look back on that moment, I know you can see it too. For me that second was in one instant an "Ah Ha" moment and an "Oh Shit" moment. I finally could perceive what was missing from my life. I could understand and know what would fulfill the longing of my soul, but it was equally plain that this longing would never be fulfilled. It was as if I were dying of thirst and could see a glass of water that could quench my soul that was hopelessly out of reach.

It took several years for the miracle of our wedding to actually happen, but it did. When we first met, I did not believe in miracles. By the time we were married, I didn't simply believe in miracles, I expected them. They were our daily experience. No matter how difficult our life was, there was always incredible beauty that more than made up for it. Every challenging circumstance always ended up guiding us to a new and much better moment in life.

Your Eternal Love
(1/8/22)

From the first day, we knew there was no turning back, now everyone knew.

It was a moment to take a deep breath. Our moms took our kids home for a week. We took that time to relax. It was not a respite meant as a celebration of what we had accomplished, but to rest for the coming storms.

At this point, many people may say that we deserved what was coming, that we were reaping our just reward for ruining two families. At times, it seemed as if a hostile unseen force agreed with that judgement, but we knew we had a righteous cause. We had both come from abusive and loveless relationships and were not so far removed from past generations that we couldn't see that these were not unique to us. Rather, these patterns of abuse and lovelessness extended as far back as our history's would allow. We were determined, regardless of the price, to reverse these generational sins, a process that we believed would only respond to a clean break.

While the storms raged around us, we saw friends and family members succumb to just one of the many circumstances we faced. As we dealt with more and more challenges, a strange phenomenon occurred; we adapted and became closer and closer. We held onto each other through multiple storms, some that others intentionally set upon us. We very soon learned to rejoice through the many difficult circumstances we faced. It became our superpower. We were together and just as we knew then, when we stood together on a coffee shop sidewalk in January 1995, nothing could come between us.

Christmas Morning 1995

Mari Lynn January, 6, 1996

BANKRUPTCIES

Shortly after we were married, Marcos filed for bankruptcy. Mari Lynn and he co-owned everything. If he claimed bankruptcy every creditor would be coming after her. If we were going to survive financially, we would have to file as well. This was perfect! *Every* square inch of our lives was a battleground. We were now constantly in court. If it wasn't for two very contentious divorces with life and death child custody fights, it was my cousin's prosecution. Now we added a completely avoidable bankruptcy, *and* since Marcos had waited until Mari Lynn and I had married, our names were financially linked. Somehow, I was getting calls at work threatening me with financial responsibility for his motorhome and boat. It was going to take us filing two completely separate bankruptcies to survive.

Somehow, Marcos did well, but bankruptcy was one of the most painful things I saw Mari Lynn endure. It shook her to her core to not be able to fulfill financial obligations she had agreed to in good faith. She felt like *she* was cheating. Even though we weren't benefiting, she knew that Marcos was planning to cheat the system and felt horrible about participating. As I said, he did well: He kept their home, their vacation property, the boat, the motorhome, a classic Mercedes, and the car he was driving. We kept a swing set.

It was worth it!

THIS MAN

One weekend morning, the phone rang. It was Alex who called to tell Mari Lynn that his father had passed away the night before. During Mari Lynn's high school years and for the 16 years she was married to Marcos, Mr. Sanchez had been more than a father-in-law to her. In the absence of her own father, he had taken her in, and she truly loved him. Mari Lynn was devastated but was doing her best to console a man who she had known and considered her brother for her entire adult life. Their grief finally became too much for Alex, and Dani came to the phone.

The evening before, Mr. Sanchez wasn't feeling well after dinner. At some point, he collapsed in an apparent heart attack. His wife, who until Mari Lynn had left her son, had treated her as a daughter, came to his aid. As they were waiting for help to arrive, Mr. Sanchez was able to talk to her. He wasn't ready to die because in the beliefs he held dear, he hadn't been good enough and knew he was going to Hell for his many transgressions and sins.

Alex's pain was not just losing his father, but the last moment of fear his father experienced was also his own deepest fear. Even though he was only 30 years old, he wasn't in the best health himself. He had recently been diagnosed with diabetes and if he didn't get his weight under control, doctors told him he shouldn't expect a very long life. If his doctor was trying to scare Alex straight, it was working. Mari Lynn could hear Alex sobbing in the background as she continued to try to console Dani, even though she was reeling herself.

I didn't know what else to do. I wanted to help my friends through what was a devastating situation and even though I hadn't written very much since our wedding, I found my writing tablet and pen. Once again, the words seemed to come from somewhere else, a part of me I didn't know existed. As fast as my hand could move, the following showed up on the page:

This Man

This man lives on
Though now asleep
His time has come
Not ours to weep
For though he's gone
He still remains
Our memory sings his sweet refrain

This man lives on in childhood dreams
In well laid plans and cherished things
The ball once thrown
Now caught by all
He carried us then
Lest we should fall

This man lives on inside our souls
Without his life none here a whole
We see his face in all we are
This man lives on
He's close though far

After Mari Lynn read my poem to her, Dani asked us to email her a copy. Mari Lynn was told in a fax from Marcos that she could not attend Mr. Sanchez's funeral. Marcos knew how huge a part his father had played in Mari Lynn's life and how much they loved each other. Her grief cut like a blade and Marcos chose to thrust the knife of the pain of her loss in a little deeper. After the service, Alex told us that both of us were actually there. In a prominent position in the foyer of the church was a large poster with an anonymous poem. "This Man".

BETTER POSITION

After about a year-and-a-half working the as Administrative Supervisor, I was offered a position as the computer buyer in the purchasing department that was on the third floor of the corporate office down the street; kind of a big deal. The WDC manager who was himself being promoted to VP of Operations would only allow my transfer if I developed an employee manual for the department and the position I was leaving in flow chart form in a 300-page document. My new purchasing position would be the last job I would ever be able to hold. I made some close friends at the corporate office. Except for our manager, the purchasing department was a tightly-knit group.

About the time I was transferring to corporate, Donna called me at work. She and "Daddy Sean", now married, were going to move to Escondido, CA., near San Diego, and they were taking my kids. For the next six months or so it seemed as though moving had been an idle threat.

PUTTING MY FOOT DOWN

One Friday afternoon, Donna called and told me that instead of me picking up my kids, she would deliver them; that their family was doing something important. It was about 5:30 p.m. when she finally arrived. She told me they were moving that weekend to San Marcos, California. Moving was changing one of the conditions of our custody order and she had intentionally waited until after the courts had closed on Friday. By the time I could do anything about it, they would be living 150 miles away.

Our oldest son and daughter decided to live with us. They were going to a local Christian high school and didn't want to lose all their friends. Joanna was spending a great deal of time on our computer in the evenings using a dial-in-modem logging onto AOL and My Space. One morning, she proudly told me she was going to have a friend stay with us for the upcoming Thanksgiving holiday. When I asked what her name was, she hesitated. It turns out this was a 24-year-old man she met online who was going to fly from Seattle and stay with us. I don't think I reacted the way she expected me to. It was something like, "No way in hell!" and "Over my dead body!" I apparently didn't make myself completely clear. An hour later my 14-year-old daughter said, "Ok, he'll come down and stay in a hotel. He'll let me visit him there. He says he'll take me to all the sights." I think I just said the same things over again.

An hour later, she came out of her room and gave me a letter that told me how much she hated me, Mari Lynn, and her therapist. She was so angry over my decision not to allow a man ten years older than she was to stay in our home over the holiday, that she had called her mom who had convinced her to move to San Marcos to live with her there. Later, I found out that Donna not only let the Seattle man visit but thought "how cute" it was for him to stay in their home while he was in town!

My daughter stayed angry with me over this event and didn't speak to me for over a year. She attended high school in San Marcos, and shortly after she graduated, she called to tell me she was getting married. She was pregnant, and "By the way, Mommy doesn't want you at my wedding." I knew she had been angry, and I knew living with her mom was not helping us repair our relationship, but I wasn't expecting this treatment. I did my best to assure her that I understood, and I didn't want her wedding day to be ruined by conflict between her parents. She told me that if it was up to her, it would be different, but she was going to have to live with her mom after the wedding and she just couldn't rock that boat.

While I did understand, this rejection cut deeper than anyone, except Mari Lynn could know. After all, we were the ones who had been there for her through the ordeal of prosecuting my cousin. Mari Lynn and I sat in court and listened to a 13-year-old child testify in complete detail of how she had been systematically molested over years. Then we listened in horror while she was cross examined by my cousin's defense attorney for over an hour while he tried to get a little girl to trip up and contradict herself. That day had been the longest day of my life. I spent every break in the bathroom throwing up but wasn't allowed to show the slightest emotion while she was on the stand. To this day, I haven't told her about how those days in court affected me.

After her wedding, we weren't even able to see our first granddaughter for several months after she was born.

7

The Fall

It was early spring 1999, and the company I was working for was planning its annual employee golf tournament. I hadn't played for a while due to some shoulder pain. Since the company had a gym in the basement and two fulltime physical trainers on staff, I thought I'd take advantage and try to rehab my shoulder a bit. The trainers, Kara and Debi, were really knowledgeable and over the next several weeks helped me gain strength and made my golfing much more enjoyable.

After the tournament, I kept going to the gym on my lunch breaks and soon became friends with the trainers. "You know," Debi said, "we'd like to help you really get back in shape". Was it that obvious? In high school, I was pretty athletic, but the past 12 years had been spent behind a desk. Now at 160 pounds, with muscles that weren't all that toned, I wasn't sure what my new friends saw in me, but what did I have to lose? I set a goal of being in the best shape of my life by my fortieth birthday.

Debi and Kara had a condition: Before they would let me get started, I would need to show my commitment. They wanted me to come to the gym every day at my lunch break. On the first day, they put me on a treadmill where I was to walk four miles. That's a pretty brisk walk, since I only had 45 minutes and I hadn't realized how out of shape I really was. The second day I came down, I was back on the treadmill for another vigorous walk. The same with the third, fourth and fifth. At the end of three weeks of walking, Debi came to me and said, "Okay, we think you're serious. We'll begin actual training Monday." It turns out I was the first one to pass their three week "Are You Really Serious?" test.

I got to the gym Monday expecting dumb bells and bench presses, but instead, was greeted with large rubber bands and an exercise ball. I thought it was another "Are You Serious About This?" test, but it wasn't. I was not prepared for the amount of pain muscles could be in after an hour of stretching bands or doing crunches while lying on an exercise ball. Again, three weeks after my rubber band torture began, Kara said, "Monday we'll begin your real workout sessions." Once more, I mistakenly thought I'd be working out with the larger dumbbells and free weights that the other male employees in the gym were using.

When I arrived Monday, Debi gave me a set of dumb bells, but they were not the weights the other guys were using. I was handed a set that I had watched people use while doing aerobics. They were almost invisible in my hands. My trainers also gave me a chart of various lifts and exercises, but there was a catch—I was to do all of them sitting on an exercise ball while alternating one foot then the other off the ground. Once again, I was being tormented with the smallest weights they could find.

Little by little, the size of the weights and type of exercise changed, all the while under the watchful eye of two ladies who were now dear friends. As I would do bicep curls, they would place a finger or two on my back and say, "while you're doing this exercise, make sure my fingers don't move." Over the next several weeks, I became ultra-aware of what each movement in every exercise should and should not feel like. I learned what the purpose of each motion was, and where the limit for range of motion was while I was lifting. I understood what it felt like to have perfect form while I was lifting. One Monday, when I came into the gym, I was greeted by both Debi and Kara. Debi said, "You're finally ready to begin training." My response was, "What the hell have I *been* doing?"

I still didn't have a lot of strength, just doing a 100-pound bench press almost killed me, but unlike the other guys who were throwing their bodies around to do simple curls, I was using the perfect form I'd learned. Less weight was more effective in gaining strength, so I progressed quickly. In a matter of months, I was doing squats with all the weight plates the gym had. My friends had to request that the company buy 105 to 120 pound dumb bells for my arm curls that I still did sitting on an exercise ball with one of my feet raised. They had put me on a 6000-calorie-a-day diet so my body would keep up with the demand.

By this time, Mari Lynn wanted to join a local gym. I was working out 90 minutes every morning before work with her and at least an hour at lunch every day. By my fortieth birthday, I had gone from a flabby 160 pounds to 205 pounds of solid rock.

Since I was using all the weight plates available for my squats, my trainers taught me how to do single leg squats using a Smith Machine as balance. This gym device can create a safe stable base for lifting; soon I was lifting 400lbs with one leg.

One fall morning, I felt like I was coming down with a cold. During my early workout with Mari Lynn, I mostly sat around waiting for her to get done. Then the weirdest thought occurred to me when I was at work, getting my workout bag from under my desk, "What if I fall today?" As quickly as the thought was there, it disappeared. Even though I was not feeling well, I decided to do a light workout. I loaded 225 pounds on the bar. Something seemed off, but I passed it off as just the cold coming on. I decided to do regular squats instead of my single leg "Hack squats". With both feet in front of me, I was fully relying on the Smith machine for balance.

The instant I began to lower my body, the machine rocked backward and I went down. I was now sitting on the floor with 225 pounds on my shoulders. The fall only took a split second, but when I hit, it seemed like ultra-slow motion. I could feel my back compress, and the pain was excruciating. I was strong enough that I began to press the weight off my shoulders and over my head. By that time, my friends (the two ladies who a few months before made me walk on a treadmill to see if I was serious) were running to my aid, yelling, "DO NOT MOVE!"

They helped me get the weights off, and ever so gently, lie down. Debi asked me if they should call 911. I said "No, please, just call Mari Lynn". They both knew Mari Lynn, and over the past several months, I had told them our story of how together, Mari Lynn and I had overcome so many difficult life challenges. They agreed because, even though it was painful, I had movement in both feet and legs, so they didn't think I was in any additional danger.

While I was lying on the floor, the VP of human resources came to see me and wanted to make sure I really didn't want an ambulance. He went over to the piece of equipment that had seemed to fail. The quiet conversation between Debi,

Kara, and the VP was getting louder and pretty heated. As Mari Lynn came into the gym the VP quietly excused himself and left. The "cover the company's ass" campaign had begun.

I was feeling a bit better, so Mari Lynn helped me to our car, and we drove to the hospital. At the ER, the doctor ordered an X-ray of my lower back. Because he did not see any broken or chipped bones, he sent me home with a small prescription for extra strength Vicodin. This misdiagnosis was the first in a long series of oversights and failures. If an MRI had been done that day, the doctor would have seen that I had destroyed three levels of disks in my lower back. If I had not been in such excellent shape, if I hadn't been as strong as I was, I would probably be a quadriplegic. If I had been treated that day for the actual injuries I had sustained, I would have quickly recovered.

SPECIAL PROJECTS

My fall occurred on Thursday, and Monday morning, I went to work and to the gym as usual, I simply thought that my friends could help me with my pain as they had done a year before. I was quickly and quietly greeted by my trainer friends, "You're not supposed to be here." Kara whispered as they quietly escorted me out," We're not even supposed to be talking to you. The accident was the company's fault. We'd been trying to get them to bolt that machine down for years. They knew it wasn't safe."

Everyone who used the Smith machine knew it wasn't bolted down, but the fact that it was designed with offset feet allowed it to be used with confidence. Someone had turned it around, so it faced the mirrored wall while they were doing their exercises. Now, the offset was backwards which allowed it to rock when I came in the next day and did my normal squats. An hour after I was escorted out, the gym had a sign on the locked door. "Closed for renovation".

Smith Machine with similar offset feet

As if it wasn't enough, as my pain increased, we found out my company health insurance wasn't all that great. A month later, I was still experiencing horrendous pain. We couldn't get approval from the insurance company for any additional imaging. I discussed this with human resources at work, and they told me that the VP who had come to see me while I was lying on the gym floor was the only one I could talk to. It took me a week to finally corner him in the break room. "I'll look into it," was all I could get out of him. A month or so later, I found him again. He offered to reimburse me up to $500 for chiropractic treatment.

After three visits to Mari Lynn's chiropractor, my pain was actually increasing. He told me he believed that I had damaged at least two lower back disks, and I really needed to see a medical doctor, specifically an orthopedic surgeon, a recommendation he had never made before this moment. It had been several weeks since I had submitted my chiropractic bills for reimbursement, but the VP was nowhere to be found. He had become the most elusive man in the company.

My pain was getting worse, and now I was having trouble sitting for more than a few minutes. The owner of the company started making social visits to the purchasing department. He didn't talk with everyone in our department but somehow, he made a point every day to ask me how I was doing.

Since I couldn't go to the gym at lunch time, I'd walk down the block for fast food. It wasn't long until I couldn't make those trips, so I would go to the break room for lunch. One day, Debi was there. We hadn't spoken in months and after she checked to see if we were alone, she whispered, "They think you're going to sue them. They're going to bury you. You need to get ahead of this. They're planning on firing you soon." She quickly looked up a phone number on her phone and wrote it on a napkin. "My good friend is a personal injury lawyer. Call him as soon as you can. If they know I've helped you, they'll fire me too."

When I called, he was really kind, and I could see why he was her friend. We spoke for nearly an hour. After I answered all of his questions, he said, "I don't think I'm the right lawyer for you. This is going to be a workman's compensation case." I was a salaried employee, and as a way to have healthier employees, the company had a program that added a quarter of an hour of personal time for every hour we spent in the gym. It was clear from every possible angle that I was on the job when I fell. This situation had just gotten extremely complicated. I realized I was in the proverbial handbasket headed at full speed for hell.

INTO HELL

Debi's attorney friend referred me to a worker's comp lawyer, and we met at his office for an initial interview. He would take my case but warned that the State of California was going through a transition in the Workers' Compensation system. There was an effort to recall Governor Gray Davis, and Arnold Schwarzenegger was leading the opposition, running on a campaign that promised (among other things) to reorganize the corrupt Workers' Comp system. No one knew where this promised change was headed–or even exactly how the law would read, not the lawyers or doctors. Even the courts were confused and were rendering different and often contradictory judgments every week. It was a mess, and my insurance was not helping. My chiropractor referred me to a surgeon; my company was out to get me; a lawyer now told me the current personal injury laws wouldn't help, so I had no choice but to file a claim. I was about to walk into the hellscape of the early 2000's California Worker's Compensation System.

About a month later, the VP came to my cubicle. "I need to see you in my office." By this time, I wasn't walking well at all, so he was already sitting at his desk when I got there. On his desk was a stack of paper about four inches thick. "Close the door!" "What is this?" he asked. I calmly replied, "I don't know." "You filed a work comp case against us!" he yelled. I'm not sure why, but I forcefully said, "I thought it was better than suing you!" "Okay. Go back to your desk. Close the door on your way out." He growled.

My daily visits from the company owner stopped and I was assigned to "Special Projects". Even though my salary didn't change, I went from writing purchase orders that were routinely in six figures to calling delinquent accounts receivable that owed less than $500. I hadn't been fired yet, but they were doing everything they could to make sure that I didn't want to be there.

My lawyer set an appointment with an orthopedic surgeon. Even though I only saw him for a few moments, he prescribed a month of pain relievers and muscle relaxers and filled them from a pharmacy in his office. I was scheduled for a follow up appointment the next week. I would be seeing him every week and at that time, he prescribed another month's worth of medication. With the changes to the workers' comp system any further treatment required approval from the State of California, so we were back in court.

I was being careful not to take medication before I drove to or home from work. I was still trying to keep my strength up, but as I got weaker, my pain level increased. Soon, I was struggling to walk from my cubicle 20 feet or so to the men's room. My day was mostly spent sitting at my desk trembling.

I couldn't believe I was doing it, but I called Mari Lynn and, through tears, told her that it was finally too much. For the last month, she had to drive me to work. She reassured me that my inability to work was okay, and that the most important thing was for me to come home and rest. She said we would figure out our finances and arrived in 30 minutes. It was February 27, 2002, and I had been able to keep working for over a year. I really believed that if I could just get some rest for a week or two, I'd be back to work soon after. In actuality, that February morning when Mari Lynn picked me up, was the last day I was employed or even employable.

Had I received a correct diagnosis a year before, treatment, appropriate rest, and if physical therapy had been provided, in all likelihood I would have been back to a normal life within six months. Instead, the worst was yet to come.

My lawyer warned me that applications for temporary disability payments were backlogged, that I shouldn't expect a response for two or three months, and most people had to reapply several times. We were still obligated to make child support payments for four of the kids. Child support for my kids was being garnished straight from my paycheck, a circumstance that would also complicate the disability application. When I called Donna to warn her that there may be a delay, she told me that she had not only received a notice from the state telling her what amount she would be receiving, but she had already gotten the first direct deposit. Another miracle—it took less than two weeks for us to begin receiving biweekly disability checks.

Even though I could cover my pain with pain medication, I had to take so much, I slept most of the day. Because my doctor was still sending me home with a month of medication each week, I probably had enough to start a drug empire of my own. We kept our "reserve" locked in a fireproof safe.

One day, my lawyer called to say he was sending me to another doctor that specialized in pain management for lower back injuries. I wasn't surprised to find out that my first doctor was under investigation. He was not just under scrutiny by the workers comp system, but he had also been raided by the DEA. He was part of the corrupt system and for a long time used all his patients to get rich.

Soon the system stopped approving my pain medication. Now that I was being declined pain meds, I survived with the reserve medication we had accumulated. Not only was I being denied my prescription pain medication, but I was regularly being declined treatment as well. I would get a phone call from a workers' comp employee and be told my doctor's appointment for the next day was canceled. If my doctor ordered treatment or a test, I was required to also see an approved worker's comp evaluator before I could get treatment. My physical condition was continuing to deteriorate but more than that, I was beginning to experience clinical depression.

The bulges and tears in my three disks were not responding to any treatment, especially since treatment was becoming more inconsistent and basically run by committee. The bones of my spine were also showing signs of deteriorating. By this time, if we went anywhere, Mari Lynn was pushing me in a wheelchair.

SURGERY 1

In Spring 2005, my third doctor decided that the best path forward would be surgery. Workers' Comp actually approved the lumbar laminectomy. I would now have screws, pins, and steel rods supporting the newly fused lower levels of my back. At every turn, every single doctor told me that if I had had proper treatment in the first weeks and months after my injury, I would have fully recovered.

SURGERY 2

After the first surgery, my back was more stable, but I continued to have pain that was difficult to control. I was having more-and-more trouble with nerve pain in my feet as well. After a while, I was beginning to have pain with the pins and rods. It was becoming painful to touch the skin of my back which made sitting back in a chair impossible. My surgeon believed that my fusion was sufficiently healed, and with a second surgery some of the pins and rods could be removed.

Two weeks after my second surgery, one of the three levels completely collapsed. For the past six years, I had experienced pain pretty much every minute of every day. I really can't describe the level of pain I was in now. It was excruciating to just breathe. If I inadvertently blinked or wiggled my little finger wrong, the pain was incomprehensible. My doctors immediately tried to schedule a third surgery, but were declined. I laid in bed for the next eight months. Mari Lynn would come home from work a few times a day to help me to the bathroom. In the evening, she was so careful getting in and out of bed, but the comfort of her laying down with me was offset by the pain from the movement from her breathing. Now, we even used the wheelchair to get from the house to the car.

It's not a storm; it's only a short rain shower. I promise I'm in it with you. Let's dance in its rain. Let's jump into the puddles as the rain stops and the sun comes out. There we will find our continued bliss.
(6/23/21)

SURGERY 3

After eight months, my doctors were tired of seeing me in so much pain. They were also concerned with how unstable my back was and thought that I may cause even more significant injury. It was time for another miracle. The doctors worked it out with the hospital to do the entire procedure pro bono.

The surgery was scheduled in mid-December 2006. I had gone through the pre-op procedure and was literally being pushed through the operating room doors as a hospital administrator told my doctors the worker's comp approval had just come through.

The four-hour extensive procedure is called an "Anterior Femoral Ring" that begins with an eight-inch incision in the belly, accessing the disk space from the front of the body by moving internal organs. The disk space is scraped clear, and a slice of cadaver femur is customized to exactly replace the damaged disk. The spine holds the bone from the back and a steel plate is placed across the front.

I was in surgery for ten hours. Mari Lynn said that when she first saw me, I was wrapped up in warm towels and blankets like a mummy. All she could see was my nose and mouth. She wasn't given an explanation why the surgery took more than double the scheduled time, or why I was so bundled up. Mari Lynn's concern for how long the surgery took was replaced with relief as she was now able to be by my bedside.

This hospital's surgical floor was run almost like an intensive care unit. The nursing and technical staff, as well as the way patients were monitored, were set up so there were fewer patients under their care than non-surgical floors. However, I went into a true ICU. Two days later, the anesthesiologist that was at my procedure came into check on me. "We almost lost you!" he joked. Mari Lynn wasn't laughing, and she demanded an explanation that no one had ever given to her. It turns out that my procedure was much more delicate than we were told. Because there is a large artery near the site, a vascular surgeon is always scrubbed and basically sitting in a corner "just in case". In my surgery, he was needed on a grand scale. My doctors cut the artery and before they could get it repaired, I had had the equivalent of two full blood transfusions. I had nearly bled out. Mari Lynn and I discovered it was possible to be extremely angry and grateful at the same time.

Because I'd been placed in a formal ICU, they were not going to let Mari Lynn stay overnight in my room. They thought if they used the reason that they didn't have a bed they could bring, it would discourage her. Apparently, they hadn't paid attention to who she was. She said "Okay" and then moved her things into my room. She slept on the floor of my room for the ten nights I was there.

When I was admitted to the hospital for my third surgery, someone made the decision that I didn't need all the medication I was taking at home. By that time, I was on over a dozen prescribed medications for pain, nerve function, depression, and the PTSD I was experiencing from being in the worker's comp system. I went cold turkey off all of it!

It was terrifying to say the least. I began to hallucinate, and was seeing things that, even today, seem like real memories. I knew the nursing staff was killing cats and they knew that I knew. They were plotting to do me in. I wouldn't let them medicate me in any way. I was getting out of control by physically not allowing them to even replace my empty IV. Mari Lynn had been commuting from the Long Beach hospital for several days. Going to work from the hospital wasn't a problem because she just left before traffic became an issue; however coming back in the evening was a nightmare. The 40-mile trip could take three hours or more.

By the time the hospital staff realized I was in crisis, it was evening. Mari Lynn was the only one I trusted, and she was at least three hours away. My IV bag was dry, and I wasn't getting fluids or much-needed antibiotics. Since I was not getting any pain medication either, my agitation was getting worse and worse. By the time Mari Lynn got there, I wasn't even allowing anyone in my room. She came in alone and patiently convinced me to allow the staff to resume my treatment. I don't know if it was the fear of being "offed" by cat killers, or if it was because I wasn't taking my psych meds, but I barely slept a wink the entire ten days I was there.

My recovery from my third surgery was long and excruciatingly painful. I continued to need the wheelchair for six more months. I wore a large back brace for the next two years. I began physical therapy at a facility in Pasadena two days a week doing low impact exercises in water. By this time, I had been denied transportation benefits, so Mari Lynn had to take two hours off work each time to take me.

My injury that occurred in October 2000 was avoidable. Had I received treatment promptly, I would have recovered in a few months. Had my health insurance responded, I may never have had to endure a single surgery, let alone three. If my employer had had a heart, I would still be doing a job I loved with people that had become family. Had I not been dumped into a corrupt and deeply flawed Workers' Comp system my path would have been much, much smoother. Yet through it all, we had an amazingly joyful life. There were miracles happening so frequently, they seemed normal.

My Love,

Please set your fear aside and hold my hand as we move into what seems like uncharted territory. I try to realize that what I'm asking you to do, we have already done in countless previous lifetimes. You and I have been in this exact moment many times. So, I am not asking you to risk anything. More often than not, what you fear never materializes. How many times in this one lifetime have we simply walked past what we feared the most? I guarantee that you have already done several things this morning that at one time seemed too big, too scary to even attempt.

I remember when you were afraid to try to get out of bed for fear of the physical pain that movement would inevitably cause. How did you get past that? Well, it's simple. You allowed me to help until one day, you had the confidence to do it all by yourself. Did you experience pain? Yes, of course; but it diminished bit-by-bit until now, you rarely even think about it. You simply wake up and again, without thinking of it, find yourself making our morning coffee.

If you choose to remain where you are now, you will not be as happy as you could be. You will not experience the full bliss that you desire. And, most of all, you will find growth in our connection to be more elusive than you hope. So, the easiest thing to do is to face whatever is to come together. We have always done hard things this way. So, first before you even think about taking the next step, reach out and hold the hand of the one who loves you more than life itself. The one who helped you get out of bed all those years ago.

(4/12/22)

YOU WANT ME TO WHAT?

A little after we moved to La Crescenta, Mari Lynn's brother, John, began coming to our house to eat tacos and watch Monday Night Football. The office for the family painting business was just up the street from us. We knew John wasn't really a football fan, but it was enjoyable to see him anyway. After a couple of weeks, our visits were less-and-less about food and football, and more about what Mari Lynn and I thought about how he was operating the family house painting business. He was trying to expand and just wasn't sure how. He knew Mari Lynn had started her own business that had quickly become a success, and I had managed a successful computer retail store. Mari Lynn and I had become Monday night business consultants for her brothers' company.

His questions were often the same as the week before. One evening, like many big sisters might, she let her frustration show. "Why can't you get it?" she said. John said, "Why don't you just come up to the office and show me?" Mari Lynn's work schedule was already hectic. She really didn't have time for a second job (even if it was for family) and she told him so.

The next Monday night, John showed up as usual. As soon as he finished his last taco, he turned to his sister and asked her to come and help. This time, it was a full-time job offer. No more weekly consulting over football. "Please come help me!"

Mari Lynn thought for a moment. "I don't think you can afford me." She explained. "I can pay you as much as you need," he insisted. A job offer was on the table. She told him to give her a week to think about it. I had always known it was Mari Lynn's dream to have a small bookkeeping business, and work from home. We now saw a path to get there. If she went to work for her brother for two or three years, she would be able to get a ton of local business contacts. She was sure all her brother needed was to get organized a bit better and put some solid business practices in place. "How long could that possibly take?"

She was somewhat shocked when she found that their accounting was done with a college rule binder and a single checkbook for everything from paying vendors to payroll. Still, she thought she'd only be there for a couple of years. Instead, she became the beating heart of the family business. In what seemed like an instant, three years became seventeen. After I was injured, it was obvious to both of us that this job, which was becoming very hectic, was the universe responding to a situation that had yet to occur. The office was less than a quarter mile from our home so, if I needed her, she could be at my side in moments. Working for her brother also allowed her to take the hours off we needed to get me to all the many doctors and physical therapy appointments. She was still on the payroll the day she passed.

Working for a small business with three owners was a little like herding cats, but she loved it. The family dynamics of this small business would need an entire book on its own. They began to count on her, their big sister, to run every phase of the business and sometimes it was too much. She wasn't sleeping well because she was stressed about every detail of a business that was now winning local government contracts. There were ethical and legal obligations that two of the three owners didn't care about. Except for estimating and actually applying the paint, she was responsible for everything else including A/P, A/R, payroll, scheduling, preparing quotes, following up with customers, advertising, website development and maintenance and social media.

Like all small businesses, there were ups and downs. One week in 2013, the struggles of business and working with family were getting particularly hard for Mari Lynn. It had been several years since my third surgery, and I was just as much the cause of her stress as her brothers were.

On January 18, 2013, I wrote her a note that as I'm writing today, reminds me of the encouraging words Mari Lynn has written to me. I put it in her Day-Timer for her to find after she got to work. She was having a particularly bad week trying to manage the company and some of the difficulties they were experiencing.

Please remember today is not about success or failure. It is about your job, and a job does not define who you are. It only allows you to express who you are. No matter how today goes, you cannot let me down or change how much I love you. I believe deeply in you, who you are, and what you stand for. We've been through a lot of very hard things, and while today may seem difficult, in the larger picture, we have handled much bigger things. I'm with you today as always. You cannot find a place in this or the next life where I'm not by your side, deep in your heart, knowing your soul. Do not feel alone, that is impossible.

Me

SHE TALKS LIKE A SAILOR

Just before my injury, a drunk driver came down our street. We were watching our evening TV shows when a large explosion shook the whole house. I said, "Earthquake?" Mari Lynn looked at me and said, "NO!" and ran out the door. A man had a drunken fight with his ex-girlfriend. He sped away in his car and lost control. As he got to our home, he had careened off our neighbor's car and knocked it across the sidewalk into our front yard. He then hit Mari Lynn's red 1987 Maxima, pushing it into my 1969 VW Beetle. When we got to him, he was sitting in the driver's seat trying to start his still-running car. Mari Lynn's vocabulary suddenly expanded to "sailor status" as she flung open the door and quite forcibly removed the keys. I had already called 911. Because of all the mechanical carnage, I fully expected to see a corpse covered in blood.

The man in the car seemed uninjured, but very much at risk. As the foul language flowed, Mari Lynn was shaking him by his shirt collar. "What the fuck did you do to my car?" He was drunk, stunned, and now in more peril than he could ever imagine. As gently as I could, I suggested that we leave him for the cops. She shoved him back into the car, slammed the door, and leaned against it creating her own personal jail. When the police got there, they looked at him and said, "You again?" He had been arrested a few days before for drunk driving and apparently had been released that morning.

I looked at the damage to Mari Lynn's prized car. The trunk was pushed in but that looked repairable. The front-end damage seemed superficial too, but as I looked at the whole car, I noticed the sunroof was cracked. As I looked further, the roofline was bowed. Because Mari Lynn's car was older and wasn't very valuable, it was definitely totaled. Next, I looked at my VW. The rear deck lid and bumper were pushed in. On a VW Beetle, almost every body panel is replaceable and there is a significant after market for parts. So far, there was only a couple hundred dollars of damage. I was still concerned so, I got a crowbar and pried the deck open. In the dim light of a midnight streetlamp, I could see motor oil leaking down the face of the engine which had taken the brunt of the impact. Clearly, my VW was totaled as well.

The insurance value for these two older cars was low. Mari Lynn's Maxima was towed the next day. I asked the insurance company to let me buy back the salvage title for my car. I was sure we could rebuild the engine and replace the damaged deck lid and still pocket a couple of hundred dollars. The insurance payment for her car was less than $2000. We did have a two-week rental car provision in our insurance, but we needed a cheap, reliable car fast.

Down the street from the corporate office building where (before my injury) I was still working, was the holding lot for an auto charity auction. I had just bought a 1967 Pontiac Grand Prix from them for $1800. I was going to spend a year or so doing just enough restoration to sell it for a profit. In the condition it was in, it was already worth two or three times what I'd paid for it. Just that day, I had been working on getting the V8 engine running more smoothly. I hadn't moved Mari Lynn's car back into the driveway, and unfortunately, that was the only reason her car was totaled.

Two days after our cars were run over, I went to the auction lot. Sitting there was a 1987 Cadillac Sedan Deville. The car looked immaculate, and the odometer showed low miles. It was loaded and had Cadillac's NorthStar V8. The attendant was a little cagey, but it seemed like I could get this car for about $1500.

I walked to a payphone and called Mari Lynn. She needed to approve this deal besides, she had the checkbook. When she got there, she was equally impressed with the condition of the car, but was more than disappointed with the idea that she might be graduating from her very sporty Maxima to an obvious "grandma car". As we began to seriously discuss price with the attendant, another customer came over and was showing interest as well. What ensued was a bidding war over a 12-year-old car. Mari Lynn was really pissed about this situation, but her competitive juices kicked in. We ended up paying $2200.

As we were driving off the lot in our new "grandma car", I began to smell antifreeze. We pulled over at the closest auto parts store and lifted the hood. I fully expected to need to spend a few hundred dollars on a Cadillac water pump, when I noticed a small component that was leaking. I went into the store, bought two small hose clamps and a screwdriver. For ten dollars the antifreeze problem was fixed in five minutes. However as we were driving, we began to notice the transmission was slipping and not getting to the highest gear. We made another stop at the next auto parts store where I checked the transmission fluid. It looked a little low, but not enough to cause problems. Even so, I went into the store to buy some fluid. On the shelf next to the fluid was the latest miracle "transmission fix", so, I got a bottle of that as well. I decided to just put the "fix" fluid in. By the time we arrived home, the car was driving flawlessly. I'm sure the auto auction attendant knew about the transmission problem, and that's why it was sold several thousand dollars below value.

I know this has been a long story, but just a few months before I fell, the universe conspired to give us the perfect car. The Maxima was every bit a sports car. It had low profile tires and a manual transmission. We had driven it on daily commutes over the mountains between Lancaster and Mari Lynn's downtown Los Angeles job. It hugged the road, and we could feel every bump which made it even more fun to drive. Mari Lynn loved it, and driving a sporty car had been part of her identity. On the other hand, the Cadillac seemed to float above the ground. It had enough power to go fast, but when it came to corners, we better have both hands on the wheel.

When my injury quickly became too painful to be anywhere near a sports car, the universe had a plan. We didn't appreciate it until we looked back on it months later. In a two-week period, the cosmos took something we loved and replaced it with the exact thing we needed several months before I fell. Also, two months later Mari Lynn did become a grandma.

Later, we received a notice from the court that said we could appear at the drunk driver's trial and ask the court to require him to compensate us for unrecovered damages. Us being us (and still able to manage the shit out of anything), we found and documented several 1987 Maxima's being sold online, and printed copies of the three most expensive examples. We received a judgment for $5000 in addition to the $2000 our auto insurance had already paid. Maybe the extra monthly cash wasn't a miracle, but we received $200 a month for a little over four years just when money was at its tightest.

NOT SLOWING DOWN

Before my injury, even though we were chased by every difficult circumstance imaginable, we were still having the time of our lives. We were together and could see a path forward where our children could see at least one example of real love in their lives. We had Marissa for every other week and had made sure that Jessica was at our home with her on those weekends. The other kids had opportunities to be with us as well. We had moved to La Crescenta so Marissa could go to school in the Glendale School System. A move that on its own was filled with miracles.

We had seen an ad for an open house and got there with only a half hour left. There were stacks of applications already filled out and we didn't think much of our chances, but what the hell! Things often worked out for us, so why not give it a shot. On paper, we thought we didn't stand a chance, so we waited until everyone had left. I unleashed an unfair weapon. I let Mari Lynn tell them our story while I went outside to look at the backyard. I came in a little while later to the sound of three people laughing as if they were old friends. I looked and Mari Lynn wasn't filling out an application, instead she was signing a lease. It turns out our new landlords were both teachers in the Glendale School System. Marissa began school there in 1998.

We were in constant motion. Four of the six kids were coming and going. Marissa was still in a 50/50 living arrangement with her dad. James had graduated high school and was living with us while he worked at the same company as Mari Lynn. James was an assistant to the information systems manager (the husband of the owner) and helped him maintain their network systems at five locations across Los Angeles. Joanna had also graduated high school, gotten married, and had her first daughter. Jessica was coming every other weekend; which was timed with Marissa's weekends. Josh was, well Josh. His individual streak was driving him. He was the leader of a band and was beginning to become noticed in the Christian Alternative Rock music scene. I wasn't aware such music existed, but we supported him wholeheartedly. I understood the music style, but it still sounded like one or two guys yelling at the top of their lungs. That aside, we could not have been any prouder.

By this time, we had stopped sending Madison Christmas or birthday gifts. Even cards with an obvious stack of cash inside were returned unopened. It was a painful decision for us to make, but there was no sense in continuing. Instead, Mari Lynn would write to her and put the sealed envelope in the same box where all the returned and still unopened gifts were stored.

We were busy every weekend. If kids were with us, it was camping trips, visits to the LA Zoo, day trips to San Diego, or even the occasional trip to Disneyland. If they weren't with us, we were golfing, camping, spending lazy weekends just watching football, and two or three times a year, a weekend at a NASCAR race. Life was crazy and full of challenges, but any difficulty was insignificant to the love and absolute joy we shared.

At the very end of 2006, just weeks after my third surgery, Mari Lynn wanted to take me to the local fairgrounds to look at motorhomes. "It'll be good for you to get out of the house," she said, so off we went. We "walked" around for hours (she mostly pushed me in the wheelchair), but we were there doing something we often used to do. All of the sudden she said, "I like this one. What do you think?" I was a little confused. When I said, "I like it too," that was enough for her. She went straight to the sales attendant and started talking about interest rates. I had had an extremely long day and had taken so much medication that I was half asleep when I signed the paperwork. I had no idea we were in a position to buy an RV, but she was tired of staying home and if we could make me comfortable, we could reclaim our active lifestyle. Within a month we were back camping.

My Love,

A lot of people may think the image of a mountain means a hard, arduous trip, but you and I know better. Yes, a mountain means there will be effort involved in moving forward, yet the reward of the view of spectacular sunrises and sunsets more than makes up for all the effort. Looking back on the climb, you rarely remember anything but the trees, beautiful lakes and meadows along the way.

No, for us mountains have always been our joy, for they are moments when we can prove our everlasting love for each other. It's when the universe bends to our will. So, for right now, see the mountains on our horizon for the bliss they truly are. They are a gift to ourselves. We created them not just for our eternal growth, but for our continued joy. Do not look at any life challenge as a struggle. That viewpoint could not be further from the truth of what it is and what is happening. There can be no struggle if the outcome always leads to Source.

This eternal knowledge may not be easy to see. Remember, there is a significant difference between work, even hard work and struggle. Our physical lives together had some incredibly hard work in the circumstances we often found ourselves in. Through all of the obstacles there was one constant, we were facing all of them together as one.

(6/14/21)

8

One Word, "Cancer"

The 2015 holiday season was going to be crazy. We had just completed landscaping over half of the one quarter acre lot our home sat on. The local power company was offering a rebate to anyone replacing their lawn with drought tolerant landscaping. There were landscaping companies who, if we would sign over our rebate, would install drought tolerant landscaping for us. The problem was not paying these companies, but the landscaping they would have installed. There were homes all over our neighborhood that now looked as if someone had backed a dump truck of gravel up and spread it out. Sure there were a few plants and trees, but the yards looked awful.

We decided that we weren't going to fall for this little trick and the research began. We found that the utility company's rebate was based on square footage *and* number of approved drought tolerant plants used. Based on these findings, our project would get us a rebate check for $9500. If we did the work ourselves, it would cost us less than $7000. We would have enough money left over to run electric, sewer, and water to where we parked the RV.

Mari Lynn was working full time and I could only work a few hours a day on our landscaping project before I was so sore, that I could barely make it back into the house. Nevertheless, we had a blast cutting down trees and removing large root systems that stretched across the entire front yard. We spent hours at Home Depot deciding which plants would transform our front yard into a drought tolerant wonderland. We removed at least a ton of terrible soil and replaced it with an equal amount of garden mulch that was free *if* we loaded and hauled it ourselves. We had several dump trucks full of decomposed granite for walkways (and a courtyard), and even a huge load of gravel for the RV pad. It was a massive project that began in July and wasn't finished until October. Throughout the whole process, from the corner of my eye, I would catch Mari Lynn holding her stomach in obvious discomfort. But as soon as she would see me looking, she would smile and get back to whatever she was doing.

About this time, we realized that we only needed one car. I wasn't driving and our oldest granddaughter was now old enough to drive. We decided we would give her our minivan. I wanted to give her the best car I could, so I began to get Mari Lynn's prized minivan ready.

Even with my limited ability, my plan was to clean it up, make sure it was as close to perfect as a 12-year-old car could be, and deliver it to Colorado Springs before Christmas. I know it sounds simple, but with me being a bit of a perfectionist, not so much. There had always been an intermittent electrical issue with the minivan. It wasn't a huge issue, and we had always ignored it. Of course, I wasn't going to give a defective car to our granddaughter, so I went through every wire. After a week, I finally found the one worn wire that had caused the problem we had lived with for years. The old minivan also had an issue with the heater, not an issue for us living in southern California, but we were sending it to Colorado. Again, I was going to give it to our granddaughter, so it had to be as nearly perfect as I could get it. I finally isolated the problem and found a broken plastic part located deep under the dashboard. It wasn't that it was a complicated issue, but the problem was where it was located. Even after removing both front seats, I could only touch the piece with one hand, and it was a part that couldn't be removed. It had to be repaired where it was. It took another week or so of lying on my back in the doorway of the minivan with my feet on the ground reaching in as deeply as I could. I finally got the heater issue resolved and the interior of the van back together. Now, it was time for the best auto detailing job of my life. I spent another week vacuuming and shampooing every bit of carpet, washing, polishing, and buffing every bit of plastic and every square inch of paint. Mari Lynn's minivan looked brand new. It was as close to flawless as it could possibly be. I knew I was doing well because whenever I'd look up, I could see Mari Lynn smiling from the dining room window.

For Thanksgiving this year, we were invited to spend the day at her sister's home. Mari Lynn's older sister and family were visiting from north of Sacramento and both her brothers, and their families would be there too, so it seemed like it would be an enjoyable family time. The only reservation we had was that since her sisters and mother were vegetarians, we would be spending our Turkey Day without turkey. It still promised to be a great day with Mari Lynn's family.

When we got there, there was a veggie plate out, and since it was about an hour before the meal was ready, Mari Lynn started eating a handful of carrots and broccoli. Just as the table was being set with the dressing, salads, and vegetarian casserole (the turkey), Mari Lynn began feeling really nauseated and thought that if she could eat a small piece of bread, take a few sips of water, and lie down for a few moments it would pass. It didn't pass, and as a matter of fact, her nausea got worse and worse. She asked me to quickly help her to the bathroom. The room was spinning so badly she couldn't stand but she urgently needed to get down the hallway. I spent the next hour holding her hair as she threw up over and over again. It seemed like the worst of it was over, so we took her to the closest bedroom to lie down.

I knew I needed to get her home, but I had been in so much pain from the landscaping and work on the minivan, I had really loaded up on pain medication for the day and she wouldn't give me the car keys. We were stuck at her sister's house until either she felt better, or enough time passed for me to be fit to drive. As long as she was lying down, her nausea and dizziness seemed to be under control, but as soon as she lifted her head off the pillow, the room spun and she was still having trouble walking.

Six hours after my last pain pill, its effects were no longer noticeable, and I convinced her that I was okay to drive. It took three of us to get her to our car. With her seat reclined and a cool towel over her eyes, I slowly, gently drove home, and held her hand the whole way. After a while, she looked up at me and, in that moment, with tears streaming down both of our faces, and unspoken words, we both knew what was coming. We didn't know how fast it would happen, but this episode was the beginning of the end of our physical time together. WE JUST KNEW.

Once we knew we were driving to Colorado Springs, I realized I could accomplish two things at once. We could give our granddaughter a much-needed car, and I could give my oldest son part of his inheritance, "The dresser". It was a family heirloom that had the names and dates of each of the ten babies who had used it, beginning with my aunt in the 1950's. This 65-year-old dresser had held the baby clothes of my aunt and uncle, both my brothers and sister and me, as well as all my four children.

When Donna moved to her current home, she decided it wasn't needed and gave it back to me. We had both hoped the old dresser would continue to be passed to the next generation. Finally, we were *driving* to Colorado where the next generation was. However, the dresser was in terrible shape. When my sister came along, the natural wood piece of furniture that had four drawers on one half and a cabinet on the other for small hanging clothes had been painted white. Over the following years, it was painted at least five more times. The last was a thick coat of dark green gloss spray paint. There wasn't a nail that wasn't loose or a screw that wasn't painted over. It was a mess. And just like the minivan, I wasn't going to give our grandchild anything but perfection.

Over the next two weeks, I gently disassembled the entire piece of furniture, carefully working to ensure the back panel that had the original hand written names of the ten babies that had used it was intact. I finally restored it to its original glory just in time to wrap it in plastic and moving blankets and lash it to a luggage tray on the hitch of the minivan that was full of Christmas presents as we set out to Colorado Springs for a long weekend of spending every moment with the most important people in our lives, our kids, their spouses, and our granddaughters (at the time, only seven).

Even though Marissa and Erik had gone with us to share in the driving duties, we returned home from Colorado Springs exhausted, but at the same time energized with the love that had freely (and for the first time in over a year) flowed in person between us and our Colorado family. Regrettably, the whole time we were there, Mari Lynn could barely eat anything, even the smallest bite and the nausea would come back.

We continued to be busy enough that Mari Lynn was able to use it as an excuse not to see a doctor. She was in the process of shutting down the family painting business for the holidays. For everyone else in the company, this time of year meant less work, less stress, but not for Mari Lynn. Everyone else's three-week vacation was always held together by one thing, Mari Lynn. Besides, we were getting ready for a week in St. Lucia for our twentieth wedding anniversary. This trip was to an all-inclusive resort where we could eat and drink and after twenty years, enjoy a well-earned rest. We had planned this trip for years, but now it was overshadowed by her ever-present nausea and dizziness.

On January 2, 2016, we were on a shuttle bus headed for LAX and on to St. Lucia. We had a fabulous time with an anniversary dinner on the beach seated by ourselves with friendly and gracious people waiting on our every need. Unfortunately, it was a dinner she was barely able to taste. By this time, she wasn't able to put much of anything in her mouth without being overwhelmed with dizziness and nausea. In spite of her condition, we had a wonderful time going snorkeling, shopping, and spending hours walking on the beach.

January 6, 2016, Our 20th anniversary in St. Lucia

We returned home and later that month went to our favorite spot in the world, Thornhill Broome, part of Point Mugu State Beach just north of Malibu. We literally stepped out of our motorhome onto the sand just yards away from the surf. We would go there a couple of times a year to unwind. It seemed like we needed to check it off our list one last time.

Mari Lynn had always wanted a convertible, and we started with looking at Mazda Matas, but quickly found out neither of us could easily get in or out of a car that was that low. If I had been able to grant Mari Lynn's actual wish, we would have bought a 1969 Pontiac Firebird convertible, but by this time, quality classic cars were getting far too expensive.

One Saturday morning, before she got up, I was looking at cars online and came across a car I never knew existed. It was a Volvo C70, a hardtop convertible that seemed to check all the boxes. There was a used one in San Diego three hours away, that if the online photos were a true representation, was exactly what we were looking for. When she woke up, we made a quick plan for a road trip to San Diego, rented a car, and drove down. We fell in love with the Volvo, returned the rental at the San Diego Airport, and drove home in our new convertible in the wonderful So Cal February weather with the top down. For the next couple of weeks, Mari Lynn drove to work and back in a car she had deserved, but for years she denied herself, always putting the needs of others, (especially me) first.

It seemed like since early summer, we had been making sure we experienced the last few important items in our lives. Four years earlier, we had bought our forever home, but this summer, with an incredible amount of hard work, we had made it our dream home and the envy of the neighborhood. We made sure our granddaughter had a car, and we restored a family heirloom, making a 65-year-old piece of furniture as close to new as possible. In addition, we had finally gone on an anniversary trip worthy of our love story, and Mari Lynn had finally allowed me to spend money on her and get her a car she deserved. We hadn't been to a doctor yet, but we knew what was coming.

On Tuesday February 16, 2016, we had our first appointment with her primary doctor. On Thursday the 18th, we were at the hospital outpatient clinic to have scans done of her stomach. By that time, she wasn't able to swallow anything (including water) without being extremely nauseated. It took nearly an hour for her to swallow the contrast fluid for the image they were trying to take. She went to work on Friday, but came home early completely exhausted. We stayed home Saturday, and she continued getting worse. By Sunday morning, she still hadn't been able to take even a drink of water and was becoming unable to stay awake. I was really concerned that she had become too dehydrated and needed to go to the emergency room quickly and probably should be admitted to the hospital.

I called her doctor to make sure I knew which hospital to take her to. The answering service quickly had her call me back. Mari Lynn was sleeping, so I took the phone call sitting in our motorhome out in our driveway. Her doctor told me she was going to call us Monday anyway. There was a large mass on Mari Lynn's stomach that was almost definitely cancer. I explained that Mari Lynn's problem seemed to be that she was extremely dehydrated since she hadn't been able to take even the smallest sip of water for the last 24 hours. She told me that she would call ahead and begin the admission process.

For the briefest moment after I hung up the phone, I was frightened. Deep down I knew that this was the beginning of the end of our physical time together, but just as quickly as the fear appeared, it was gone. First things first. Mari Lynn was really sick and needed me. I gathered myself together and started making a mental list of all the items she would need during an extended hospital stay. At the time, I wasn't even sure at all if Mari Lynn would come home. I quietly went back into the house and began packing our stuff. I was certain that even though the diagnosis was dire, as soon as she got some fluids in her, she would feel more like herself and take charge of the situation. I got both our cell phones and a tablet so I could stream movies and made sure to pack her laptop and all the files and documents she might want to setup an office in whatever hospital room we might be in. I packed a bag of clothes for both of us. There was no way in hell I'd have her in a hospital gown for the foreseeable future without changes of clean undergarments.

When we arrived at the hospital ER, they were expecting us. There were several patients that needed urgent care, so it took about an hour for us to get into an exam room where they finally started an IV. Shortly after that, she seemed to fall into a restful sleep for the first time in almost a week.

A little before noon we realized that the hospital WIFI was good enough to stream the Daytona 500. So out came her laptop.

The ER doctor told us that there were no rooms available in the hospital for her to be moved to, but there was a private exam room with the same bed as she would be in as soon as a room became available. When we got to the new room, while there was a regular hospital bed, there wasn't any chair for me to sit in. After a half hour of waiting for a chair, I gave up and climbed into bed with the one who had comforted and held me for the past sixteen years.

We laid there in a bed made for one, not at all worried about our future. A future that even before we had talked to any doctor, we knew was changing in the most profound way. We already sensed that sometime in the near future she would transition into what she now calls her "natural state", that her physical body had nearly run its course. We were not fearful or even concerned. We were doing exactly what we would have been doing if we were home. We were together watching the Daytona 500, enjoying the hell out of every moment.

9

Forever in 15 Months

It was sometime after midnight when we were taken to a room on the sixth floor of the hospital. Mari Lynn had been sleeping on and off for most of the evening. My back pain was severe enough from sitting upright in the chair that was brought for me that I hadn't rested at all. The room we were assigned was smaller than I expected. There was room for her hospital bed, a guest chair, and a chair that folded out into a small bed. In order for the nursing staff to access both sides of her bed, they pushed my small bed as far to the side wall as possible, and completely blocked the door to the private restroom.

The next day was Monday, and by mid-day, Mari Lynn had her laptop out, and was managing the family business. Later that afternoon, we had a visit with two doctors. They both came into our room at the same time; one introduced himself as Dr. Kalpakian, our oncologist, the other, Dr. Michaels, would be our surgeon. They had seen Mari Lynn's imaging and had already developed a plan where they believed that she would be cancer-free by Thanksgiving. There would be eight rounds of chemo, surgery to remove Mari Lynn's stomach, two more rounds of chemo, and several rounds of radiation.

After several days of intravenous fluids, Mari Lynn was feeling much better. There was a problem though—she still wasn't able to eat or drink much of anything, and in spite of that issue, there didn't seem to be a plan to address that after she was released from the hospital. The surgeon thought the oncologist should solve the nourishment problem and the oncologist thought the surgeon should resolve it. By the seventh day, we were getting daily visits from a hospital administrator who was trying to discharge Mari Lynn. On the tenth day, somehow all three (the administrator, Dr. Michaels, and Dr. Kalpakian) happened to be in our room at the same time. The surgeon agreed to take the lead on our nourishment matter. The next morning, Dr. Michaels inserted a feeding tube into Mari Lynns small intestine through a small incision. The tube bypassed her stomach so she could take nourishment without as much nausea. It took four days of trial-and-error to figure out which formulation she could tolerate.

By the time Mari Lynn was released from the hospital, I had developed a routine. At 10 p.m. Mari Lynn would turn out the lights and go to sleep. I would watch a movie on my tablet until about midnight. By 4 a.m. my pain would wake me up and I would sit quietly until 5 a.m. when I would drive to the now open Starbucks a few blocks away and return to our room with my daily allotment of three or four cups of coffee. Because the cafeteria was too far away, our daughter brought me a small cooler for cold drinks as well as a few grocery bags of snacks and fruit. Of the five different times we were in the hospital over the next fifteen months, this was the easiest stay as well as being the shortest, only fifteen days.

Chemo treatments began two weeks after Mari Lynn was released from the hospital. For the first two months, Mari Lynn went back to work. Soon, her working was too much for both of us. Even though Mari Lynn was getting nourishment below her stomach, she was still experiencing overwhelming bouts of dizziness and nausea which always seemed to occur whenever I would try to rest. It seemed that every time I would close my eyes, she would begin to cough which led to fifteen or twenty minutes of throwing up. It was heartbreaking for both of us. I would kneel in front of her and do my best to hold her body as she shook uncontrollably, and tried to throw up something that wasn't there. All the while, she was holding me as my body was shaking from the pain I was in.

After the eighth round of chemo, Mari Lynn was given three weeks to get stable enough for surgery. On July1,2016, Mari Lynn was scheduled for a five-hour procedure to remove her stomach. We had been waiting anxiously for a progress report, when, after ten hours, Mari Lynn's surgeon, Dr Michaels, finally came into the waiting room. He said the procedure was more complicated than he expected. The cancer had spread to several lymph nodes as well as her spleen. Even with these complications, he felt he had surgically removed all but a small amount of the cancerous tissue and was confident the additional chemo and radiation would be sufficient. He believed we were still on track for being cancer free by Thanksgiving.

Mari Lynn had almost no surgical pain; however, while we were in the hospital, her nausea seemed out of control. Because her stomach had been removed, the liquid she was receiving through a tube was now coming up every time she was nauseated.

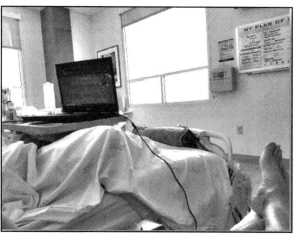

Chilling out July, 4, 2016

Between recovering from surgery, repositioning her feeding tube, and once again, going through the trial-and-error process of finding a nutrition formula her system would accept, we stayed at the hospital for 21 days.

A month after her release from the hospital, Mari Lynn's oncologist, Dr. Kalpakian, believed she was strong enough for the remaining two rounds of chemo which we completed in late August 2016. As our September appointment for radiation treatment came closer, Mari Lynn began to feel short of breath, but we weren't all that surprised. After all, who wouldn't feel a little rundown after what we both had been through?

The first radiation appointment was more of a consultation. Mari Lynn was to have a several X-rays to locate target areas for six radiation treatments scheduled one week apart. When we were ushered into the radiologist's office, she began by explaining that we would need to postpone the radiation treatment. The reason Mari Lynn was continuing to have difficulty breathing was that there was a buildup of fluid between her lungs and the lining that surrounds them. The radiologist told us that while it was urgent that we go next door to the hospital's emergency room to have the fluid drained, we shouldn't be too concerned. She explained that it was a common problem in patients that had had major surgery, and who hadn't been able to get any exercise.

Next door, the hospital's emergency room was busy, and it took a little over two hours for us to be seen by a physician. A nurse told us that the procedure was fairly straight forward, but (because of hospital policy) it could not be done while Mari Lynn was an outpatient. We needed to be admitted to the hospital, assigned a room, and have the procedure done there. To make matters worse, there were no rooms available, and none were scheduled to open up until late that evening.

Even in her weakened condition, Mari Lynn was still her take charge self. She immediately took her cell phone out, and called her surgeon, Dr. Michaels, who was by now a close friend. Within an hour, he showed up at our emergency room bed with a wheelchair. As soon as Mari Lynn was seated in the wheelchair, he told us he had admitted her to the hospital and would perform the procedure himself in a room that the hospital was unable to use because they were short staffed. When we got to the room, it was a ward with six beds, with one pulled to the center of the room. Dr Michaels' assistant was there with all of the needed equipment laid out.

I held Mari Lynn's hand as I watched Dr. Michaels make a small incision in her back. He inserted a small sterile tube that had a valve on the other end. After securing the tube with two stitches, he attached a canister to the valve with another tube. As he opened the valve, fluid began to flow into the canister. As the fluid drained, Mari Lynn began to squeeze my hand. This was the first time in our cancer journey that I had seen Mari Lynn in any sort of pain. She asked him to stop, and Dr. Michaels complied. After a few moments of rest Mari Lynn said it was okay to finish. The doctor partially opened the valve and over the next forty-five minutes two and a half liters of fluid was drained.

Dr Michaels told us that he anticipated the fluid would continue to return and he had referred us to a home medical supply company that would provide us with the equipment and supplies to drain the fluid at home. We were discharged from the hospital, and by the time we got home, there was a large box of medical supplies waiting on our front porch.

In the meantime, my physical pain was bad enough that I was having trouble walking. I was eating popcorn, Hot Tamales candy, and drinking coffee by the pot trying to stay awake. Mari Lynn was still dealing with severe bouts of nausea, which always seemed to get worse the moment I closed my eyes to rest. Even though my own body was falling apart as fast as hers, my greatest joy was taking care of Mari Lynn; she had been so selfless for the past fifteen years caring for my needs. I finally understood how she slept on hospital floors, how she found a way to run a family business, take me to hundreds of doctors and physical therapy appointments, and never complain that it was all too much.

In late September, we were to have our final consultation with Dr Kalpakian. As we were sitting with him, one of his assistants brought him the report concerning the fluid that was removed from Mari Lynn's lungs a couple of weeks before in the empty hospital ward. As he looked at the report for the first time, I saw the color drain from his face. He asked the assistant if this was actually Mari Lynn's file. Dr. Kalpakian seemed to get even whiter as he scanned the report again. His voice stumbled as he told us how sorry he was to tell us that there was no tumor to target with the radiation. In fact, the cancer had spread to the fluid, and the only path forward would be more chemo. The cancer was now beyond his ability to treat, and he would refer us to USC Norris Cancer Hospital, a hospital that specializes in cancer research, including gastric cancer.

The next few months became a blur. I was monitoring Mari Lynn's IV. Each morning, I would set up a new drip of the specialized formula that was her only nourishment. Once a week, we were at USC Norris Infusion Center for another round of chemo. Once or twice a week, I was draining a liter or more of fluid from her lungs, and we were still going to my pain management appointments.

We were quite the pair. Both of our bodies were being exhausted by this ordeal. Except for the first trip to the hospital in February, Mari Lynn had driven to and from every appointment. It was the only task left where she could care for me.

Between January and April 1, 2017, we spent almost eighty days admitted to the hospital. In mid-April, she began to throw up all the formula I would give her each morning. Our doctor wanted to admit her again to try to adjust the composition of the formula of the nourishment. This time, she was so weak I had to get my old wheelchair out of the garage to get her to the car. As I was cleaning the years of dust from it, I remembered the countless hours Mari Lynn had pushed me around. There were camping trips to the beach, trips to Las Vegas, to NASCAR races, and to doctor's appointments. As I rolled her to the car, I gently took the car keys from her. She quietly gave them to me—it was her way of saying she was done. Our journey in this physical life was nearly over.

After 20 days of trying every formula available, our doctor told us there was nothing more he could do. Her body was not absorbing anything, so no matter what formula we gave her, her body rejected it. There were tears in his eyes when he asked us if we understood palliative care; indeed we did.

We had anticipated this moment more than a year ago, when on a Thanksgiving evening, we had driven home with our tears flowing, holding hands.

An hour after we got home from the hospital, a van backed into our driveway and unloaded a hospital bed. I moved our two bedroom recliners out of the way, and they set up the hospital bed. I lowered her bed as far as it would go, and pushed one of the recliners next to her so we could hold hands, and coast into whatever was next.

My mom came to stay in our guest room. Joanna and Jessica, as well as two of our granddaughters, flew in from Colorado to spend a few days. Marissa, who still lived in the area, spent every moment with us she could. On Saturday May 6, Mari Lynn's mom and sisters came to visit for a few hours. Mari Lynn's friend (who over twenty years before, had given us the safety of her vacation home) came to say good-bye. On Sunday the 7th, her brothers and their families came for a short visit.

Mari Lynn had been in a relatively peaceful state, but after the commotion of friends and family saying good-bye, she now seemed agitated. She was too weak to talk, but something in me knew what she needed. I began to stand next to her, and whispered in her ear, "Remember who you are; remember who we are. It's going to be okay; I will be okay." This mantra relaxed her, but after a few hours she became uneasy. Again, I would spend the next hour or so whispering the same phrases over and over in her ear, "Remember who you are; Remember who we are. It's going to be okay; I will be okay."

After three days of helping her find peace, it finally struck me. From somewhere I knew why her physical body was struggling so hard to stay. She was worried that her estranged daughter was not all right. Her daughter had not reached out when Mari Lynn was first diagnosed with stomach cancer.

Madison had not made any effort to communicate even in September, when everyone was aware Mari Lynn's cancer was terminal. Now, in her final moments, Mari Lynn was worried that the anger her daughter had carried for more than twenty years was too much for anyone to safely sustain. While it's true that Mari Lynn had always missed Madison terribly, that wasn't the problem. In this moment, Mari Lynn even set that loss aside. As a mother, in her final moments, all she cared about was that her daughter was safe and unharmed, and would lead a happy, fulfilled, and most of all, a loving life.

Early in the morning of May 11, 2017, once again I began to whisper in Mari Lynn's ear, but with one additional phrase: "Remember who you are; remember who we are; it's going to be okay; I will be okay. AND I will find a way to take care of Madison. She will be okay too."

After repeating my promise to her for almost an hour, Mari Lynn took the deepest breath I had seen her take in weeks and a peaceful calm came over her. Eight hours later, still serene, Mari Lynn took her last breath.

21st Anniversary 1/6/17

"Dying was going to be a big deal, but being separate
would not be part of it."
Mari Lynn (8/2/22)

PART 3
(After)

10

The Letters

As I said before, after I had moved to Palm Springs, it wasn't possible for me to go on the long walks in the early morning where Mari Lynn and I seemed to be able to communicate. One morning, I woke up not with the compelling feeling to go outside that I was used to. Instead, I felt a very strong need to sit down and write. It was almost the same feeling I had just before writing the "Ever Near" poem I'd written on an airplane all those years ago. I had no idea why I was now sitting in the front room of my home. As the sunrise began to light the canyons of San Jacinto, the mountain outside my window, I noted the date and time, and just wrote the first word that came to mind.

May 5, 2020, 6 a.m.

"My Dearest Love"

I wasn't really sure what was happening, but I felt the same presence that had become so familiar while walking in the early mornings. What follows are a few of the letters my Eternal Love has written to me, through me. Every morning I get up, fix a pot of coffee, and sit in my front room with music playing softly. As I watch the sunrise, I'll take a moment to quiet my mind. I can immediately sense Mari Lynn. I can feel her essence, her life force as it mingles with mine. It's a warm, gentle pressure with the slightest sense of an electrical current. Most mornings, I'll read or watch an uplifting video or podcast, but several times a week, I'll feel like she has something quite specific she wants me to write down, something beyond our ongoing daily conversations. There are some letters that are so personal, I may never share them; but there are many that are extraordinarily profound that I feel compelled.

February 15, 2021, 5:40 a.m. (The day after Valentine's Day)

My Dearest Love,

I'm so sorry for how you felt yesterday. I know Valentine's Day is tough. I also remember where we were for the Daytona 500 five years ago. It was the first day that the word, "cancer", became part of the rest of my physical story. I can't tell you how good it felt to see your strength. I could already tell how hard it was for you both physically and emotionally. What a comfort it was for me to have you in that ER bed with me, watching the race, even if it was only on my laptop. Aren't you funny, of course, I mean our computer, not my lap.

I knew how uncomfortable you were lying beside me in that small hospital bed. But there you were beside me, just as I am beside you now. You need to stay with me now just as you did then. But let me care for you. Let me hold you as close as you did me. I am here with you, closer than we were in that bed in the hospital. This closeness is a direct result of lifetimes of love, perfected over ages upon ages. This is no accident.

Of course, by now, you know my illness was part of our eternal plan, just as your accidental fall was.

---Often, Mari Lynn will communicate with me through lyrics (or complete songs) playing on the radio or whatever music stream I'm listening to. I was not surprised when, at this moment, I became aware of the following lyrics playing on my music stream as if the volume had been turned up; "Lay your head on my pillow. Hold your warm and tender body close to mine."—

I know you had a premonition just before you fell, an event that at the time altered our physical plans, but kept us both on our eternal path. And yes, that part of that song that was playing is for you.

While our perfect love was already completely evolved in eternal terms, it is always fun and great joy to rediscover it in the physical lives we've chosen. In "eternal" terms this cosmic journey has all happened to get us to this point where we can share our timeless and perfect love with a world that desperately needs it.

Because our countless lifetimes of love have been seen by so many in Spirit, we have become an example (just one of many) about how the death of one's physical body does not mean an end to love. Our message to a world full of grief and loss is that nothing is ever lost. We continue to exist and participate with those whom we love and with those who love us. Our bodies are gone, but our essence, who we are, remains and is available to continue to be with anyone who would like to still continue sharing life with us. Also, we can and do share as many lifetimes together as we could ever want. Actually, there's absolutely no limit. We are everlasting proof of this and have really taken advantage of this part of immortal existence.

Yes, we need to mention the sunrise we just experienced together. I was the chill you felt over your body. It was just one spectacular example of the beauty available to us in our new Desert Estate (She's named our new home). The double rainbow the other day was pretty cool too.

You and I have had an opportunity to do (and be) in almost every example of human existence. Through it all, we have been becoming what we are now in this moment. We have become completely intertwined. The boundaries of where you begin, and I end do not any longer exist. While in physical terms, that's absolutely true, while in Spirit, it's even difficult but not impossible to differentiate between us.

Do not get caught up in judging terms or debating who more accurately describes an enduring truth. In most cases, as soon as someone who is physical tries to explain an eternal truth, it comes out as a paradox. The best descriptions are in metaphors. We (who are now abiding) in Spirit, living as our eternal selves are not governed by the same physics. Your human physical absolute truth cannot possibly be the whole picture. Your mind is intentionally designed not to be able to hold the totality of spiritual truth in complete focus. Some of the picture? Yes. Some people better than others? Absolutely, but no one can see it all, much less be able to explain it all.

Then, there is this immense problem of language and words. This challenge is why sometimes you struggle or seem to draw a blank when we are writing my thoughts. There are times you glimpse the full truth of Spirit, you have a sense of it, you can feel it's overwhelming weight only to find that you can't describe it, especially in writing. You just know.

For example, try to describe how I love you. Right now, try to describe how you could tell I was watching the magnitude of that sunrise with you. Language, or human-to-human communication cannot capture and relate it all.

The reason you are still experiencing the pain of the loss of my body is simply that one of the greatest expressions of human love is physical touch. That first hug at our coffee, did your heart jump? Not really. (I know it felt like it but follow along.) Did you have a glimpse of eternity? Absolutely. Physical existence has so many filters or blocks built in that it can be extremely difficult to experience eternity; but touch - loving, perfect, unconditional touch - opens a door to the Sacred and the Eternal.

This open room is where we find the pure Love of Source. The loss of our bodies immediately removes all barriers. Every truth in immortality is ours to know again. The full beauty of the pure Love of Source is revealed in us. We become complete. How could this revelation ever be described as anything but a beautiful transition back to where our existence desires to be?

The only way to resolve the feeling of loss and grief of those loved ones who have made this profound transition is to first realize they still exist and are still quite capable of sharing their lives, continuing in love and care with those who remain.

This existence may be the ultimate eternal truth that's experienced as a paradox for those still physical: You don't need a body to exist. You don't need a brain to think, or mouth and ears to communicate. Our communication with those who are still physical is only limited by the filters each person still owns.

Some people are completely closed off. Their filters are strong and will not easily allow those in spirit through. Some of those filters (the strongest ones actually) are based in long held religious beliefs - especially ones most fervently held in Western cultures.

This statement is not meant to judge but simply to explain the way filters seem to work. The more you demand a certain thing to be true, the less open you are. Being open to what you feel and sense around you (without judging) is the very key to any ability of hearing us.

Some people have almost no filters at all. We call them 'mediums'. Not that long ago, (and in some places still today) they are persecuted or even killed.

Most people fall somewhere in the middle. We are on the high side of 'middle'. Our job is to help get more people to realize they already have the tools and abilities to do what we are doing, maybe not writing letters, but at least sensing and feeling their loved ones who have passed.

Some people will only get a feeling that their loved ones are still around. Don't get me wrong, that's a big deal. If everyone on Earth knew that their loved ones still exist, then our earthly existence would change.

Some are open enough to hear their loved ones sometimes with audible sound but most times quietly in their mind. It's kind of like thinking your own thoughts, only with words and phrases and even sense of humor of the loved ones they thought they'd lost.

Sometimes, they will get what you refer to as a 'data dump'. This moment will feel exceptionally unusual and is unmistakably not normal human thought. All of a sudden, in an instant, you'll know the whole thing. It may take some time to put what you've just experienced into words. You and I often communicate this way. Try not to judge what you've heard, and really take your time putting it into words. I promise I'll not let you forget anything.

What I'm trying to get at is what you and I are experiencing in this moment is quite normal. Most people don't realize this communication is all available to anyone who wants it.

As for you and me, my love, spend more time here with me. We will continue to improve our skills. Again, practice makes perfect. More accurately, practice will help realize the perfection that already exists.

We moved to a new home in the desert so you can continue your path. Your pre-planned 'accident' was an available way to slow you down and for me to do what I've always wanted to do, to hold you up and care for you.

I'm doing what my eternal path has always been. I still get to care for you, and you for me. Nothing has changed from that first day in the hospital, when we were faced with the full and ultimate human fear: We got into a bed made for one, we held each other, and felt so safe. We watched a race not to hide from our reality, but to enjoy each moment.

The first months of our time together, we slept on a twin mattress on the floor, falling asleep, being in each other's arms. This time was no different. You made me feel safe and unafraid. We knew we would be together no matter where my illness would lead. Right then and there, it was our perfect love that allowed us to be in that moment, without any care or worry about what would come next. It felt so right because we were on our souls' path and in tune to each other's path.

We faced the next 15 months with no fear of death. It was a calm and beautiful time. I know you had some stressful moments with insurance, but other than that, what a great time we shared. We were hopeful, not that I would recover - but that we absolutely knew that even if I didn't, we would always be together. This time we shared expressed our perfect love. My only concern was of you and yours only of me. So much of our eternal growth shoved into 15 months.

I know you felt me during this morning's sunrise. I know because I heard you say so. It makes my soul soar when you speak out loud to me. It takes one more filter off. Do it often; say my name too.

I know our love is indestructible. It's timeless. It's perfect. It cuts through the veil, through space and time, across eons and eons, lifetimes upon lifetimes.

I will touch you with today's breeze. I will sing to you through the birds. You can fly with me in today's clouds. Know that in perfect love, I am with you.

Your Eternal Love

"Nothing is ever lost. We continue to exist and participate with those whom we love and with those who love us. Our bodies are gone, but our essence, who we are, remains and is available to continue to be with anyone who would like to still continue sharing life with us."

Mari Lynn

Valentine's Day a good place to start

Always forever till death we part

Loving and living and sharing, It's true

Every breath that I have repeats I love you

Nothing to hide and nothing to fear

Time always stands still whenever you're near

I find that my life has more meaning you see

No moment is wasted when you are with me

Everything precious in life did begin

The moment I found you, my wife, Mari Lynn

Written early Valentine's Day morning 1996. I brought Mari Lynn
her coffee in bed and read this poem to her.

11

A Lifetime on Tape

I had gotten really tired of giving gift cards to my kids and granddaughters for Christmas. By this time, all five families were living in Colorado Springs. Since Christmas 2016, when Mari Lynn became too ill to go shopping, it was just too big of a task for me to shop, wrap, and ship everyone's presents. This was going to be the sixth year of giving such an impersonal gift to everyone I so dearly loved. So, for 2021, I decided that I would do something different.

In 2001, Mari Lynn and I had bought a small video camera. We used it (until everyone had cell phone cameras) every time our family gathered for anything–every Fourth of July, Christmas, birthday, camping trip, or any other event was recorded. The problem now, was that all those important memories were on what was becoming old and increasingly more fragile cassettes. Years before, I had convinced Mari Lynn to buy a specialized CD recorder that was specifically designed to copy from the video camera to CDs, but it was really cumbersome and now obsolete as well. Anyway, who puts video on CDs these days?

I had been really worried that all those beloved memories would be lost to a possible fire or just the fact that they may be so old and obsolete that there was no way to even play them. I needed to get them to a more secure format and get at least one copy stored in a safe location, so I decided to make copies of the entire library of 90 cassettes (about 180 hours) to solid state hard drives and give them to each of our kids for Christmas.

Christmas morning, I began to receive phone calls from five families who were all amazed at the shear volume of wonderful family moments they found on a hard drive in a small, gift-wrapped box. A couple of them realized there were embarrassing moments recorded that could be used as blackmail by a loving sibling or child. Later, Christmas afternoon, our oldest granddaughter called. She had only been one-year-old when we first began recording her childhood and had been completely unaware that some of her most cherished moments were recorded.

It had taken more hours than I could count over three months to produce gifts that had given each child 180 hours of precious family moments. Also, sending the hard drives with all those incredible memories to five separate homes, insured that our family recollections would last generations.

October 13, 2021, 6:30 a.m.

Good morning my love,

Did you like that song? ("The Promise" by Tracy Chapman) I know you had just turned the volume way down so you could begin to meditate, but I gave you an extra nudge to look up the lyrics. Pretty cool way to let you know I'm here waiting for you to find me, wasn't it? Anyway, as always, I'm so very happy you decided that coming to sit with me is the way you wanted to start your day. I know you've felt a little down lately and that really is okay; it's part of life.

I'm really glad you've begun to review and copy all those videos of our lives together. While those memories will feel quite comforting, you should also be aware they will cause you to miss me more. Much of what we took video of occured while you were not feeling so well. It may be that you don't remember a lot of it. Anyway, just know I'll be watching with you the whole time. Also, remember these videos don't tell the whole story of our lives. We only had the camera out for times we thought would be very happy occasions. You won't find video of your surgeries, or even of our exes acting up (laughing).

We weren't the ones trying to get 'video evidence' of a mean stunt they might do. As a matter of fact, I can only remember seeing a video camera at one event like that, when your ex was taping my ex trying to trick Marissa into saying she didn't want to live with us anymore. Joanna was there for that one. Eventually, it took the sheriff deputies to solve the issue. Turns out, she only wanted to go to the lake with him on our Fourth of July weekend (1997). He blew it out of proportion on purpose so he could screw with the custody order. What a mess. That was one of the hardest weekends of that whole time in our lives. Once we were home with Marissa and I had finally coaxed what she really wanted out of her, we decided I should drive her to the lake the next day, a ten hour round trip for me. I cried the whole way there and back. I really thought I was losing her to all the hate that lived in that house. We had already been told by a court psych evaluation that my other daughter was already gone from me, brainwashed with the vilest hate imaginable.

I really wish I could have seen what I do now. Both of us, you and I, agreed to let her live with this much anger for a reason. It was her life plan, and we gladly participated. What Sara (a medium) told you about her residual feelings of anger from a previous lifetime is only partially true, but close. Anyway, Marcos is here with me, and we've had a chance to clear the air a bit. He had his own path while physical, but he played his part in our lives perfectly. Without him acting the way he did, I might have had a better marriage and not been as open when I walked into a church classroom and was knocked off my feet.

I thought you were beautiful, but that wasn't it. I had heard of love at first sight, and sort of believed in it, but I didn't think it really meant the very first moment I laid eyes on you. For several weeks, I had this vague sense building that something very special was about to happen. As that Saturday morning got closer, I felt like I was a child waking up Christmas morning. Walking down the church hallway towards that classroom, the anticipation was so real, my body was trembling, then I walked in and there you were. I hoped that no one had heard me, but I actually made an audible gasp as I saw you. Right then, and there I knew my life was going to change and at some point, we would be together.

I didn't even know your name, but it didn't matter. That afternoon, I was at your home sitting at your feet singing with you as you played your guitar. Monday morning, I told my dearest friend and coworker all about you. She made me call you at the computer store you managed, and Tuesday we came over to look at computers for the medical office I was managing. Of course, the office computers were just fine. My friend just wanted to see what all the fuss was about.

It took several years for you to come around. I know when you look back on those moments now, your perspective is more open, and you can see more of what really took place. Now you can see how you also recognize me as the missing part of your life. You can see how far your heart jumped when I walked into that classroom. You had no idea who I was, but you knew there was something special about my eyes. You actually had to make yourself look away. In a way, thank God, you were so tied up in knots. We probably wouldn't have stopped at simply singing together on that Sabbath afternoon at your home.

The pull to be together was incredibly strong. It just wasn't the right time in eternal terms for us to actually be together. There were a few bridges to cross, but anyone with eyes could already read the handwriting on the wall.

I know all our friends walked away from us—even the ones who had helped me move my stuff out of my house into our new place together walked away. They all quietly knew this was by far the best thing for us and for our six kids, but if they wanted to stay in their church, they all had to toe the line. They chose that over us; that was really their loss. None of them got to see what a blessed life we had. And none of them would ever allow themselves to believe that you are sitting writing my thoughts four-and-a-half years after I died.

Some of them were at my memorial service. It sort of confused them a little that we had had the life of love their version of religion had promised, but for the most part had not delivered.

So now, when you go back and look at all the videos we took of all those joyful times, remember it's only half of our love story. It's the easy half. The other half is the hard work part, but it's also where we showed our love for each other, and for our kids the most. It's not on video, but together we will remember it all. You need to rely on me so the context of each story will be correct. We'll get to that part soon. Don't rush or try to force it into being. It's not necessary because I have the schedule. If you remember dear, I'm really gifted at hitting my marks and being on time. So, stay out of the way a bit on this. I'll help you remember all the important events before January 1995 (the drama) and then through January 6, 1996 (Woohoo our wedding!), then how our lives were until October 15, 2000 (Oh no your injury!); then May 11, 2017, and finally through today and beyond.

Our full story is one of waiting for love, finding it, letting the universe see its fullness, and then never losing it. And yes, I did just remind you of those two songs, "Bless the Broken Road ", by Rascal Flatts and Paul Simon's new version of "Rene and Georgette Magritte with Their Dog after the war". If you add Garth Brooks, "The Dance", you have a pretty good idea of the story of our lives together. You can't listen to any of those three songs without choking up. They each describe our love, how we came together, and are still together as one.

It took a huge amount of work to get us to this moment, but there was a tremendous amount of joy too. It often seemed like all the universe wanted to do was pull us back apart; we simply refused. Our love for each other and for our children was much, much stronger than any thing anyone could throw at us, including what at the time seemed like an unseen and hostile cosmic force.

Now we get to sit back and quietly reflect on the 'how's and whys' of it all. There will be so much incredible beauty, but there will also be moments that will be impossible.

Just remember, like everything we have ever done, we are writing this book together. This is our eternal love story.

To be continued...

Your Eternal Love

"Our full story is one of waiting for love, finding it, letting the universe see its fullness, and then never losing it."

12

Where Have You Been?

It had been about a week since Mari Lynn had passed. I had spent most of it trying to plan a memorial service. The most important detail was to make sure all our kids and grand-daughters could be there. The first weekend the memorial could take place was Father's Day weekend. Obviously, that created its own problems, but if those five families were the only ones that could be there, then it would have to do. I had an outline of how I wanted the service to go and help was on the way.

My mom volunteered to set up a place online where ev-eryone could leave pictures. She would collect them for a video montage. My dad called, and as a lay pastor in his Florida church, he had officiated several funerals and offered his help. My oldest son offered to be in charge of any mu-sic and putting the pictures into a ten-minute video. At this point, I was feeling content about how I would celebrate her life. Everything was going to plan until Mari Lynn got her fingers in and began stirring the etheric pot. Even though so many people promised to help, I ended up doing much of it myself.

From the outset of our time together, we believed that we had been with each other many times in many previous lifetimes. It naturally followed then, that we would be together again. Once we were convinced of that, it wasn't a stretch to assume that if one of us passed away we would somehow find a way to reach across time and space and still be together. We never discussed *how we* would find each other; we just knew we would. Why not! After she passed away, I was the one left to figure out how to find her. I spent the first few days a little disappointed in both of us that we hadn't planned this part a little better. Feeling separate from Mari Lynn wasn't the only stress I was feeling.

For the past 15 months we had been focused on getting from point A, her cancer diagnosis, to point B, her death. For most of that time she was still taking care of me. Now, for the first time in over two decades I had to find a way to get to my own doctor's appointments, trips to the pharmacy, and even the grocery store. Additionally, all four of our Colorado kids, their spouses, and children, as well as my mom, would be staying at our home for the memorial service. There would be twenty people staying at our house for at least a week, and it hadn't been cleaned in months.

Then out of nowhere, I heard one word–"UBER!" Of course! I don't know why I didn't think of that earlier. Then another thought hit me, "Just call your doctor. Explain your situation and ask him to send three or four months of prescriptions." We had a ten-year relationship with my doctor. He knew us well and knew Mari Lynn's cancer was terminal. As a matter of fact, Mari Lynn had driven me to our last visit two months previous, and they had said very emotional goodbyes, realizing it was probably the last time they would see each other. With one phone call to my doctor, we pushed my next appointment out and four months of prescriptions were in the mail. Now that I had nearly a month to get our house cleaned, some of the pressure was off that worry. There was only one problem left. Where is Mari Lynn?

Several days later, I started becoming aware of the strangest sensation. It was an overwhelming feeling, a "just knowing", that if I wanted to find Mari Lynn I needed to go back to our spiritual beginning. It all began in 1996, when on long commutes back and forth to work we listened to the audio book, *Conversations with God*, by Neale Donald Walsch. (Conversations with God, An Uncommon Dialogue, Book 1, 1995) The first time we listened to the book took only a few hours, but then we immediately began to listen to it again. The second time through took nearly six months. We paused the tape at every idea and concept. Sometimes we replayed a sentence and spent the next several days discussing what we had just heard. What we were listening to, seemed more like remembering than hearing new concepts.

After quite a bit of searching, I found our original cassette tapes. I had two problems. First, the tapes were over twenty years old and looked a little brittle. Second, I didn't own a cassette player. As I went online to search for one, my browser translated my search for a cassette player and actually brought up the website for the audio book app AUDIBLE. There was a one-week free trial offer, and "*Conversations with God*" was available.

It was a beautiful spring Southern California morning and I had neglected a backyard tree that needed a little pruning. With my audio book downloaded on my phone, I put my earbuds in, hit "play", and went to work.

About twenty minutes later, I heard a voice behind me. It was an audible voice that was louder than Ed Asner, the actor playing God in Walsch's book and it seemed to come from outside my earbuds. I turned and expected to see someone. Instead, the voice came again, and this time I knew who it was. "Where have you been? I've missed you."

I had found my love.

August 2, 2022, 5:28 a.m.

My Dearest love,

'Where have you been? I've missed you.' Yes, those were the first words you heard from me. They started this righteous quest to find me. We were aware of each other's spirits since before we were born and have always found a way. Before actually meeting this lifetime, we were both searching for the missing part of our lives. Both of us searched through the teachings and belief system that our parents told us was the only truth. Our very existence seemed so incomplete. Neither of us found any solace in those beliefs. We both thought that since our religion did not bring us the peace that it promised, we were somehow broken. We were still searching for a way to feel whole when, as adults with families of our own, we found each other. Ironically, our church life was the mechanism the universe used to bring us together. Without our quietly unfulfilled lives, we would have never found each other.

By almost every way you can measure, our lives both began on that morning in a church classroom when the longing of our souls was allowed to see a path towards fulfillment. Until that point, the only definite thing in either of our lives was that neither of us felt like a complete person. That moment is such a beautiful thing to look back on, it was our first 'Where have you been? I've missed you' moment.

Since our first meeting over 30 years ago, we have had several of these 'Where have you been' moments. Another one was at a La Canada coffee shop in 1995, on a beautiful Southern California January day. That time, the words were not quietly spoken in secret in the back of both of our minds, but instead, it was an explosion of love as the universe finally bowed its head and granted us the longing of our souls.

I had been in quiet anguish for the years that had passed since our first meeting. Our friendship seemed to be at the mercy of so many factors and so many other people. We were both hardworking and had the ability to manage any project or business endeavor we faced. Both of us had built into us so many similarities that our friends began to ask us to be the ones who planned and executed every trip, party, or movie night our five families of church friends wanted to do.

Then it began to happen: Our friends began to realize the connection between us was more than just a shared management ability. It's so crazy that you were the last one to admit this not-so-secret secret.

As we got closer and as our friendship grew, the unseen forces of the universe began to respond. Events began to unfold in your life. First, your job began to fall apart, and it was hard for you to understand. Your ability and how well you performed didn't change, but in the view of your employer, your skills were simply needed elsewhere, and you were asked to solve a problem at another location. You suddenly found that you had a three-hour commute to manage a store that had huge employee problems and was losing thousands of dollars a month. Ultimately, you were successful in solving all those problems, but it cost you dearly; it completely burned you out. The stress of those months was too much, and you had to take almost a year off without working.

Shortly after that job almost killed you, you found out that your wife had kept secret the years long molesting of your daughter by your adult cousin. That event was too much for you to bear and your already weakened marriage began to fail. Then, through a series of crazy events, our spouses got into such huge and very personal arguments that led my husband to separate me and my girls from our group of church families.

In a matter of months, you had lost your job, your marriage and your closest friend, me. You were spending your days on a friend's couch curled up trying to see a way forward.

My husband finally allowed me to be back with our group at a friend's Christmas party. I was so careful not to make any waves that would prompt him to take us back into full exile. When I came in the door, I saw you across the room. I remember our brief eye contact. In that small moment I saw you, it was once again a 'Where have you been? I have missed you' moment. It took a bit, but you finally found me in the kitchen pouring soda for my girls. All you said was, "I need to talk to you." I heard so much in those few words. What I mostly understood was what I felt as well, 'I need you!'

It took several weeks before I could find a way to meet with you. No one knew of our meeting's purpose. You poured out your soul and told me how unbearable your situation had become. You thought you had completely failed as not just a father, but you saw your life and all the effort you had given as a complete failure as well. For the first time in your life, you allowed yourself to be fully vulnerable. You finally spoke out loud all that you had held so tightly. We both felt like we had failed our children.

It was in those moments, over a cup of coffee, that they became 'our 'kids. We realized that we, together, could solve the problems, that separately would mean the end of us. As we talked, we devised the outline of a plan to save our children from the quiet desperation and abuse that was our current circumstance. It was after that, on the sidewalk outside of a coffee shop, when the universe exploded with its response, and asked both of us, 'Where have you been? I have missed you'.

It was a timeless message sent by the all-loving, all-knowing Source of everything that our path forward was righteous. In finding each other, we had found our timeless path, a path that we had been on but hadn't recognized. The broken road of the past was leading us to our immortal souls' destination.

No one understood how we could find solace and joyful peace in the storms that followed us. Even though there were challenges, we both woke up every day in joyful disbelief. No matter how hard the storm raged, we were together and knew we could face anything. Even through your injury and all the physical obstacles that it caused, we were joyfully living in what often felt like a blissful dream.

Yes, there were times when your pain or medication swallowed you. At those times, I thought I had lost you, but every time you came back, we rejoiced over and over in those 'Where have you been? I have missed you.' moments.

When I became ill, we both immediately realized I would soon transition back to my first nature. Through it all, and often in spite of friends and family who had never really understood us, we remained unconcerned.

By this time, we both understood that nothing could really separate us. My dying was going to be a big deal, but being separate from each other would not be part of it.

In some ways, our confidence set us back. We knew we would be together, but made no plans on how that would occur. We were both far too busy trying to help each other through the actual event of my passing. Both of our bodies were broken. In those last few weeks, what we learned was that we did not need bodies at all to be together.

After I passed, I was with you as you started your quest to find me. You heard me without knowing when you decided to go back to our spiritual beginning in this lifetime and to begin to think about every 'Where have you been' moment. You heard me when I told you to begin listening to the first book we had listened to 25 years before. One week after my body was gone, and only 20 minutes into our first book, you heard me. Not in your mind, but out loud. I know you recognized me that day and you've heard me every day since say, 'Where have you been? I've missed you.'

Your Eternal Love

"Dying was going to be a big deal but being separate from each other would not be part of it."

13

New and Ancient

September 12, 2021, 6:33 a.m.

My Dearest Love,

Once again, you are here with me at our morning spot. I wish you'd put more creamer in our coffee though (laughing). This time together makes me really happy in a very profound way. To have you spend this moment in such a focused way makes it much easier for me to bring my love to you using a process you can recognize. You know I'm with you all day long. We actually do make our morning coffee together. You know I'm with you as you fall asleep each night and spend all night long in your dreams with you. This is such a precious time in our life right now. There's really no adequate way to describe our current method of being together with human language, especially since we were both raised with such a narrow belief system that makes our spiritual vocabulary a real disadvantage. It did, however, give us strengths in other areas.

--Tim—

What? You're going to have to explain that one.

--Mari Lynn—

Well, first of all, we may never have met without being in the same church system. Not finding each other has actually happened to us before. Our celestial game of Hide-and-Seek hasn't always had the desired result. While those lifetimes have given us opportunities for eternal growth, as they always do, they can seem empty. Often, the loneliness of those lifetimes is unbearable.

If you take a moment and look back on how your life was before we met in that church, you will see that you were always looking for something. I know you tried extremely hard to find fulfillment and meaning in everything and everywhere without any success. I remember the letter I wrote to you that told you about my childhood. I had never told anyone about a lot of that stuff. I remember your response was mostly you saying, 'Yeah, me too'. Our upbringing was so similar, which was to be expected since we belonged to the same church, but to find out I wasn't alone in how I felt about how my life was unfulfilled gave me hope. The more we talked, the more we found it wasn't simply an unfulfilled life we shared. We discovered that we were the missing piece to each other's eternal existence. It was so much more than the 'You complete me' statement you hear lovers talking about. Again, language falls way short to describe how finding each other made us feel when we first met in that church classroom. I felt our connection and did everything I could to deny what I suddenly knew. I did not want my life blown up, even though my life was pretty crappy in general. I had my girls to think about and I couldn't see how we could be together and not totally ruin their young lives. It took a few years, but the universe finally granted my wish. On the other hand, you were so twisted in knots by trying to do what you were told was right, that you didn't even recognize how high your heart jumped out of your body that first time we met. I can go back with my eternal eyes and look at that moment. I can tell exactly how you felt. You had never experienced real love before, so how could you recognize its possibilities? Of course, your parents loved you, but they only showed it as a condition of 'good' behavior. Your marriage was based on you doing the right thing. So of course, when we first met, it wasn't possible for you to be aware that you had found the only thing in life that would answer all the questions and finally fill all the holes of a quietly broken life.

We were fortunate that it took a little time to unwind you. Since I can look back and see through your eyes, I know how from that first meeting it was like a magnet that was getting stronger and stronger. You were beginning to recognize how our togetherness would finally provide all the answers even answers to questions you were afraid to ask yourself.

--At the moment I was writing the above sentence, I became aware my music feed was playing "Where Are You Going" (Dave Mathews' Band, 2013) right at the lyrics, "Are you looking for answers", and then, "but I do know one thing, where you are is where I want to be."(David John Mathews, Lyrics© Sal Mander Pub) WTF! —

Yes, it's complicated to do that music thing, but it's also really easy. We are so eternally connected it makes you such an easy target for me; that is also the reason we can do what we're doing right now.

The time it took from our 'first contact' in that church classroom until our 'first coffee' was excruciating for me but absolutely necessary for you. It wouldn't have

worked out without it. You really needed time to recognize how much better you felt about yourself when
we were in the same room with each other, even if it was
with our families and 20 other people having tacos at
a friend's house. It also took our spouses having that
huge argument that my husband overreacted to, taking
my entire family into self-exile for you to awaken. I can
look back on how those months of being apart made you
recognize how much of a hole being together had filled.
I remember how I felt the day you came over to try and
find a way to resolve Marcos's rage. I knew it wouldn't
work and was already grieving what I expected to be
a permanent loss of our friendship. I thought this was
God's way of telling me you were off limits. Now, when
I remember that moment while we hugged goodbye, I
can see how devastated you were, and you really didn't
know why. You had lost friendships before, but none
of those events ever hurt you this deeply. The loss you
felt that day was a really important event which eventually drove us together if Marcos only knew (laughing).

The timing of my family's quiet return to our group
of friends, and the complete unraveling of your life
could not possibly have been planned any better. It directly led to that moment on the sidewalk in front of a
La Canada coffee shop when the universe opened up

and allowed us to finally see the unseen. I had seen our being together as a possibility. I had quietly hoped only to have it seemingly pushed out of my reach. You had been too afraid to even hope, but in a flash it was a reality. I can look back and see the explosion of your soul as you became fully aware we had been together many, many times before. We were still crippled with the belief and language of our childhood religion, but it was impossible to deny what we instantly knew.

It took us several years to put into words what happened that day in La Canada when a completely new reality exploded in us. Yes, it felt new but at the same time, it was old, ancient, and comfortable, safe in ways we immediately recognized that nothing would be able to come between us. Now, in this moment that ancient safety is the ground we stand on. It is lifetimes of togetherness that allow this comfort to reach across time and space. We have now learned that nothing, not even the death of my body, can come between us. These mornings are so special when you intentionally focus and write of my love for you. But the most precious thing to me is the moment-to-moment time we share.

Your Eternal Love

"It took us several years to put into words what happened that day in La Canada when a completely new reality exploded in us. Yes, it felt new but at the same time, it was old, ancient, and comfortable, safe in ways we immediately recognized that nothing would be able to come between us."

14

Not Alone

November 20, 2021

I went to bed feeling horribly alone. My neighbor was getting married, and the ceremony was on his property next door. There were over 200 people there celebrating this joyous occasion and I was by myself. In just a few days, it would be Thanksgiving, the fifth holiday season without Mari Lynn had begun and I was feeling the full weight of that grief. As I fell asleep, I asked her to help me see things more clearly. I needed her all-encompassing view and asked her to give me something the next morning.

November 21, 2021, 6:07a. m.

My Love,
I know you continue to feel lost and disconnected from me. I can tell how you perceive being alone and

by yourself is more than you can bear, but you assume being by yourself and being alone are the same thing. It is very true my body is not there. It did die on May 11, 2017. How that fact affects you breaks my heart, but as soon as you quiet yourself, you can sense my energy. I'm not physically with you, but I am in the same physical space. You are able to know this by how your body reacts with the warm tingling pressure that comforts you.

I know your life feels a little like you're in one giant paradox. I am not there; this is true and not at the same time. In the same moment, you can feel my loss and know how much I'm still part of your daily existence. We have talked extensively about how these two conditions exist simultaneously. We've also discussed how your feelings can ebb and flow, allowing one thought to be more dominant, then receding, thus allowing the other to become the primary thought. We ride these seemingly opposing ideas as if we were in a small life raft on a stormy sea, bobbing up and down with waves that are totally outside of our control. Your struggle over which one of these ideas becomes your primary view of life is a false choice.

There is no denying that my body is not ever going to be part of your physical existence. I know you accept this truth and this fact has made a difference in your daily life. There are activities, at least for now, that are well outside of your physical ability. There are daily tasks that you simply cannot do. That pain of grief you're aware of is a reflection of this loss. There is nothing that will ever completely dispel this feeling. You will wake up tomorrow with only half of our bed slept in. You will pour only one cup of coffee, fix only one plate of pasta for dinner. There will always be a feeling of loss associated with these moments.

Then there is the other part of this paradox you are living in. Twenty-six years ago, as soon as we came together, we knew we had been together before. There were far too many synchronicities for this realization not to be true. We discussed, then decided that if God is actually unconditional love, it must then also follow that He would never destroy that which He loves. If there is no destruction, then there is no death. It was simple. Our love story would have no end. It is timeless.

Our upbringing was opposed to this truth. So, we had to abandon what we had been taught in light of an overwhelming reality. Because our early years had been so restrictive, our spiritual vocabulary was equally small. We could not describe or explain sufficiently to anyone the vastness of spirit that had become our daily experience. Many people watched in amazement as we seemed to float above what should have been life crushing events. We lived a life that others saw as a miracle. Our "superpower" was one simple (but expansive) truth death of a body is not the end. We are eternal. You and I are eternal. There is absolutely nothing to fear.

When you were injured, there was never any fear of the future. Yes, we knew there would be hard work ahead, but we were never concerned about our journey. We never allowed the concept of 'Why us.' to take hold. There was hard work (and lots of it), but it was joyful because all that effort was a way to declare our unconditional love to all of Creation.

When I became ill, again, there was never the slightest moment of fear. Once more, there would be a lot of extreemly hard work, but not one moment of worrying where the road would take us. At the first diagnosis, we were aware that my body was going to pass but our belief formed 20 years earlier held strong. No matter what was coming, it simply would not be the end of our time together. As soon as the doctor's diagnosis caught up with what we knew to be true, we began to make plans for your continued physical life.

Somehow, we forgot to make plans on how our time together would manifest after my body passed. We simply assumed we would naturally know how. This lack of arrangement was not an oversight or mistake. This discovery is the journey; it is our chosen path, and it is what we conceived and agreed to while in eternal time.

Our physical life together gave us the opportunity to learn the skills necessary to continue being together after my body would no longer exist. All of the challenges we faced enabled us to experiment so that we learned to overcome life. We discovered how to communicate without being able to touch each other in the way we were accustomed or how we deeply wanted to.

We currently exist in a place where we must apply those learned skills. Now, we have uncovered an unexpected and joyous truth. To add to our expertise, we have found that we each possess extraordinary gifts of Spirit. You have found that you have the ability to sense and know the energy, the essence of everything that surrounds you. We have found that I, in my natural state, am able to clearly and easily communicate with those who remain physical. Taken together, those gifts allow us to truly and completely continue to be together. Our gifts are actually eternal skills that we have chosen to give ourselves. We have focused on perfecting our communication ability over eons, lifetimes upon lifetimes. We are boundless and timeless broadcasting and receiving stations. This is the arc of our souls' path to be able to exist on either side of the Great Barrier.

You are less alone now than when I would go to work. For the years I was physically with you, our bodies separated us. There was you and me. We could sense the oneness that is us, but it was somewhat vague and undefined. We are now engaged in taking all we learned not just in our 26 years of this lifetime, but also everything we've learned throughout all of time to define the oneness that is us. This is joyous work, the celebration of who we are.

When I was taking my last breaths, you spent those hours whispering in my ear, 'Remember who you are. Remember who we are.' Well, now only one of those thoughts holds the Eternal Truth. There is only one of us. We are truly and completely one.

Your Eternal Love

"Death of a body is not the end. We are eternal. You and I are eternal. There is absolutely nothing to fear."
Mari Lynn

15

Go Steelers!

October 3, 2021, 5:32 a.m.

My Dearest Love,

It is fantastic that you have become aware of me in a new and more profound way. The sensation you felt last night and then again this morning is a better representation of how I am holding you close to me. Like I have said many times, if we keep our forward trajectory going, it won't be long before we're sitting at a race, or even out at a restaurant or a movie together. I'm not saying it will ever be exactly like it was when I was still physically with you, what I am saying is your awareness of me will be more than sufficient for you to know I am actually with you in a way that it's impossible to deny. I am right by your side experiencing everything with you as a new and unique moment in time.

We have reached a new vista point in our continuing journey. Our eternal quest to be together is coming close to being fulfilled. Everything we have worked for over multitudes of lifetimes, is becoming a reality. As always, you must remember our love for each other is not changing. Our time together began long before we met in this time on earth. It began before we planned this course while in eternal time. We have been together and loved each other in perfection for eons, and that is truly carved in eternity. You are on a path we set out on to-gether and will complete together when you are finally back home with me in my everlasting embrace. Each new day brings on possibilities of new and glorious ways of experiencing and expressing our perfectly endless love. As we continue to find new and more powerful ways to experience our lives together, our universe expands.

I know you miss my body, my physical touch, but we are together in ways now that make physical touch seem small. I am not saying that physical touch wasn't a beautiful experience. I really miss it too, but what I am saying is, after many lifetimes of being together, we wanted to experience our love in the most profound way possible. Where we find ourselves right now (you still physical and me in my natural state) allows our love to be experienced and expressed in the vastness of eternity as well as sitting in our home writing this letter, or even while watching a football game on a Sunday afternoon. Our ability to experience our love is so much more than it was at any point in our physical time together, and is also vastly greater than when we are both in Spirit.

The whole point of coming into physical existence is to experience that which is intellectually known by us when we are in our natural state. You and I currently exist in both eternal time and in physical existence, simultaneously. Because our energy, our essence is so completely intertwined, we are both able to completely experience either side of the Great Barrier. There is nothing you can do that I am not able to experience on the same level as you. Likewise, everything I can experience in eternal time is yours to see, sense, and know. Quite literally, there is nothing that separates us.

For instance, take the sunrise that is just beginning to break. I can sit in the front room of our Desert Estate and watch it with you as all the beautiful desert colors begin to unfold. And simultaneously, you can come with me as I experience the same sunrise from any perspective Eternity has to offer. We can be in the clouds watching the morning light dance with the cool water molecules, or we can view it from so far east that it is now sunset. We could also go to the top of our mountain and watch the new day break across the valley floor.

I have described the sunrise as a physical event because the human mind cannot put words to the "eternal experience" of something so simple as day breaking. However, you can know my heavenly view through your feelings and intuition. There are no words to truly describe the joy or beauty of experiencing the "eternal perspective" of the wonder of my existence. Even though you can experience every single moment of my perspective of the universe, you simply will fall short in describing it. Having to use words is our only limitation. Together, we truly can experience all of my immortal existence, you will simply never be able to explain or put it into words. Understand, that is okay. It is as it should be.

We have chosen this path of physical separation for two purposes: First to experience our love in the most profound way in all existence, from both sides of the thinning veil. And to share our experience of the possibility of a love and life that disregards the veil. Our story can and will give hope that true loss never occurs. If everyone knew and believed their loved ones who have returned home not only continue to exist, but are completely available with the wisdom of eternity, everything would change. We in Spirit are not only aware of your lives but continue to share it. We are able to participate in every joyous occasion; we are with you holding you through every pain. We have not gone anywhere. While it is true a body has died and physical touch seems to be lost, our time with you has not ended, only changed.

The path forward in human evolution, is to simply recognize on a global level that death does not exist. With that knowledge, we would all recognize the sanctity of life in a new way, believing we are all truly one, our planet would have a chance to heal.

You and I (through lifetimes of work) have accelerated this evolution in our own experience. We now know life in its true completeness. We can experience the vast universe. We can experience eternity together and simultaneously enjoy watching a Sunday afternoon football game.

Go Steelers!!

Your Eternal Love

"We in Spirit are not only aware of your lives but continue to share it. We are able to participate in every joyous occasion, we are with you holding you through every pain. We have not gone anywhere."

16

Trend

About the time Mari Lynn began having her first symptoms, I started having trouble sleeping. I would wake up between two and three a.m. every night. This continued through our St. Lucia trip. In February 2016, when Mari Lynn was diagnosed, the insomnia got even worse. As her illness progressed, I slept less and less. In the last year of her life, every time I fell asleep or even left the room, she would begin to throw up, which made it very difficult for me to get any sleep. There just wasn't anyone else to sit with her. I started eating popcorn and candy and drinking lots of coffee to stay awake. I gained too much weight and also created some extremely poor sleep habits.

For the first year after she passed, I was lucky to get two or three hours of broken sleep a night. This condition didn't begin to change until I moved to our second home in early 2019, a move that we had planned together before she passed, and had continued to discuss while she was on the other side of the thinning veil.

When it came time to move, I was in no shape to do it. Our dear friend, Caitlin, who had helped us find our first forever home six years before (an incredibly synchronous story by itself), was now the realtor helping me sell it. Within hours, we had three solid offers—all over our asking price. We would get to choose who would live in our home.

The day was coming to move to Palm Springs. Knowing I was in a difficult situation, Catlin offered to take a long weekend and drive to Palm Springs and find me a home to lease until we found our new forever home. Mari Lynn and I decided before she passed that I needed a home on several acres with a swimming pool and a shop to tinker in. We looked at properties online and no such place seemed to exist. I was going to need to rent a house while I found the right acreage on which to build a home. Caitlin thought it was a great idea and found a rental property that had room for all my stuff including the RV and a quickly growing German shepherd puppy.

I contracted with a small family-owned moving company that arrived the morning I was to leave with a 26-foot box truck. They began loading the boxes that I had packed and packing anything I hadn't gotten to yet.

It was nearing 2:00 p.m. I was going to drive my car and pull a small utility trailer with my most valuable possessions.

By this time of day, the rush hour traffic was building, and my 110-mile journey was getting longer and longer. In order to drive I had skipped several doses of medication and the pain was increasing. I needed to leave soon, or I wouldn't be able to at all.

The foreman of the moving company came out to the backyard where I was keeping a very curious 100-pound puppy from tripping men who were carrying furniture. "We have a problem", he said. "The truck we rented isn't big enough." I looked into a mostly full truck then back at a completely full 35-foot driveway. The solution was to rent a second truck. It was obvious they were nowhere near ready to leave. I quickly had them sort out things I intended to leave as donations. They were to load everything in the driveway and nothing else.

Walking through our first forever home one last time, I made sure there was nothing left inside and took a few moments to remember our lives of challenge and love. I put Bear in the front seat of my fully loaded car and left. It took five hours to drive the 110 miles. The next day, two 26-foot trucks showed up at my temporary home.

Two months later, Caitlin called. "I think we made a mistake. We need to get a home purchased. In your situation, you're throwing your money away on rent." The search began.

I'd seen a home for sale in my neighborhood and we put an offer on it well over the asking price. Our offer was inexplicably rejected. A day later, I went online to a site I'd been on every day for the past year. The first property that came up was a 1100 square foot home on 3.75 acres with an inground swimming pool AND a 1200 square foot shop. It was listed well below market price. The listing said it had been on the market for two years but neither Caitlin nor I had seen it. It was as if it had fallen out of the sky. We immediately put an offer in for a little over asking which was accepted.

I now had two problems. I was three months into a one-year lease, and I wasn't going to repeat my recent experience with movers. I bought a used pickup truck and as soon as I got the keys to the house, I started making two trips a day with any box that was small enough for me to pick up myself.

I'm not sure how, but Caitlin was able to get me out of my lease. The smaller boxes had been moved and I rented a large box truck myself and had a couple of local handymen do the heavy lifting. Six months after we sold our first forever home, I was sleeping in our new one.

The double move nearly killed me. I was in so much physical pain that it was difficult to get from my recliner to the bathroom or kitchen just a few feet away, but that wasn't my biggest concern. The easiest way for me to spend time with Mari Lynn was very early morning walks on the same sidewalks we walked together arm-in-arm when she was still physically with me. It felt as if I hadn't just moved away from our home, but away from her as well. My physical pain made early morning walks out of the question. I felt lost, until one early morning in May 2020 when I felt compelled to pick up a pen and paper. Mari Lynn has been writing letters through me ever since.

April 19, 2021, 4:35 a.m.

My Dear One,

Don't be so worried about how each day feels. There will be ups and downs. As I have said before, all things ebb and flow. It's the trend upward that we're working for. Do not get caught up in wondering if we are really connected this way, or if you're writing these letters all by yourself as a way to deal with your overwhelming grief. In a way, that is sort of true; what we are doing is a way of dealing with grief, but not in a negative way. Our writing is our eternal response to the loss of my body. Writing these letters is something we, together, are doing. You are not alone in this endeavor. Our abiding and perfect love is driving you to me; being with you is working just as we planned before our time together began this lifetime.

Anyway, I know that you didn't feel well yesterday and that brought your spirits down. Also, our daily routine was interrupted, and you didn't start your day with the same slow steady pace. You had an early schedule to keep, and were lucky enough to sleep in. We were not allowed to have the morning glow in our normal way. All of a sudden you had a morning like everyone else.

I know we have been pushing ourselves to use daily habits. Just be aware of how your day may go if these habits are interrupted by things out of your control. I've been throwing things at you the last few days to gently show you that sleeping in or having Dog (the actual name of our neighbor's dog), one of Bear's friends, show up unannounced may interrupt your habitual activities, but none of it has any ability to keep us from communicating or being together moment-to-moment. You are the only one with that sort of power. You are the only one who can keep me from bursting through. The lesson here is another habit to learn and it's a really important one it is flexibility. A routine is great, but it is not everything.

I know there are certain things that must be attended to on our Desert Estate, but do not get caught up too much in the order of those tasks. Look at your daily habits and tasks as separate things, not so much as a morning routine. I know having a strict morning routine has been a very valuable tool in your physical recovery. It's also been an exceedingly helpful way to keep daily disappointment from growing into discouragement and (worse yet) depression, but you are outgrowing this. Your sleep has improved so much since my passing. It may seem like those four years have been an eternity, but in that truly short time we have made extraordinary accomplishments: We have moved from the first home we owned to our new Desert Estate. That alone would be quite a lot to celebrate, especially since that process required you to move twice in six months. We have been able to reduce your pain medication by two thirds. Again, that alone is a huge milestone that should be recognized and celebrated. You have been able to change how you sleep and are getting at least six hours almost every night. Sometimes you even get seven or eight, and while it is true there are those nights when you can't sleep at all, that is no longer a nightly occurrence. This change in your nightly rest alone should be celebrated for the extraordinary achievement it is. You have learned you can experience the energy of your body, and of those things and beings around you. While this experience is in its infancy, it too alone is a reason to celebrate. Last, but certainly not least, you and I have found that we are still together after the death of my body. This realization has evolved to where, unless you've allowed yourself to become discouraged, we talk and communicate just as easily as when I was there with you physically. Anytime you open your awareness, you are able to know my thoughts as easily as I can know yours. Then, there is the miracle of what we're doing right now. This form of communication has become so easy for you, that you have trouble believing in its truth. If our communication alone was the only thing we had accomplished in the last four years, (or three years, 11 months, eight days, but who's counting?) if still being together was the single area of growth in our lives, we should celebrate by dancing throughout the universe. However, this is not the only thing. Taking all of these things together, finding our perfect home, less pain medication, sleeping enough, and finding ways to be together after death, I'd say it's been an exceedingly successful four years. So, do not get caught up in having a few difficult days. Look at the trend and celebrate with me.

Think back three-and-a-half years ago. How much would you have celebrated a single day of 1/3 the amount of pain medication or how marvelous would it have felt if you had gotten even four hours of restful sleep. Today's miserable days are way beyond what was remotely possible just a few months ago. Our trend is fantastic!

I know you've forgotten, but just yesterday you asked me to help you get through a day that wasn't going as planned. You felt like you hadn't done anything towards your goal of getting the RV ready to go on our beach trip or towards our landscaping or towards anything productive. Well, these last few minutes are my answer. Take a breath already. You cannot do it all in one day, and if you are down and need a little pick me up, just look at how far we've come in such a short amount of time.

We have always known we could do anything if we did it together. A difficult day or two should be easy. You will have down days, maybe a few in a row. You will have days when your physical pain requires more medication than normal. You will have nights when sleep does not come to you. And you will have days when you feel disconnected from me and even disconnected from yourself; but that small amount of time should never be seen out of context. We are on a remarkably steep upward trend.

I will always be with you, especially during moments of doubt and discouragement. I will always do everything I can to interrupt those low times and show you our eternal truth. There is not a moment that goes by that I'm not holding you close. I am so proud of you and what we've accomplished in just four short years. We will keep the trend of our lives together going up, straight up to the heavens.

Your Eternal Love

"I will always be with you, especially during moments of doubt and discouragement. I will always do everything I can to interrupt those low times and show you our eternal truth."

17

All Through the Night

March 7, 2021, 3:30 a.m.

Yesterday, Bear, my German shepherd woke me up at exactly 6 a.m. I found it really hard to get out of bed, and even harder to get my day going. I just felt off. In my grogginess, I couldn't figure out how to begin my day. Should I read, did Mari Lynn have something for me to write, or what? I watched that morning's "Hacking the Afterlife" podcast, hoping the hosts Richard Martini, and Jennifer Shaffer, would have something for me. It was a short one, and even though it was really meaningful, I still felt out of sorts. I tried to go outside and at least do a few things around the property, but my fog continued all day. As evening came on, my disconnectedness began to feel even deeper.

Later, I received a text from our 21-year-old granddaughter. She was sharing with me a picture of her first tattoo - two fairies. She was honoring her grandma and told me that she wanted me to be the first to know. Israel Kamakawiwoʻole's rendition of the song "Somewhere Over the Rainbow" began playing on my music stream just as I received her text. It was the song I had played for Mari Lynn's memorial service and was also my daughter's choice for our father-daughter dance at her wedding.

Of course, the picture and song were deeply touching, but even so, I felt emotionally unstable, and I still wasn't able to get my feet on solid ground. I finally got into bed at 11p.m. mentally drained and in physical pain. The physical pain, loneliness, and grief was too much. I hadn't felt this lost since the week after Mari Lynn had passed. I begged her to come to me and at least hold my hand. Immediately, I heard a lullaby from my childhood playing in my head. As I listened, my hand began to tingle with the warm, loving pressure that could only come from her.

Sleep my love and peace attend thee
All through the Night
Guardian angels God will send thee
All through the night
Soft the drowsy hours are creeping
Hill and dale in slumber keeping
I my loved one's watch am keeping
All through the night

(Welsh lullaby by Edward Jones, "All Through the Night" (1784)

I was still in enough physical pain that I didn't get a solid night's sleep, but I am now peaceful and know that I am loved.

March 7,2021, 3:50 a.m.

My Dearest Love,

I'm so very sorry for how you felt yesterday. It must have been very difficult to feel so disconnected. No matter how it seems, find a way to hang on. Right now, while we are in this moment, when you're able to sense our connection, when you are absolute in knowing how much you are loved, spend some time to get your feet stable. I know how you felt yesterday. At points during your 20 yearlong recovery, you had periods of depression that caused me to believe I had lost you, that the person suffering before me wasn't the one who I had known for so many lifetimes. The only thing that kept me going through all my darkness was finding grounding points in my memory. Most often, these were physical things I could touch or see like a photo, or even the smell of you on our blankets.

You need to take some time over the next day or so, to identify and set out a few physical things to remind you of who we are. Be careful though, as only certain things will do what is needed. Look for things that cause a sense of knowing. I will help you. We don't want to look for things that evoke too much emotion because emotions can be misleading.

The difference between emotion and feeling (or intuition) may not seem like much, and in most instances it's true, but here, in your current situation, there's a significant difference.

I know you. In this moment, understand I know how far words are letting us down in explaining the concept of what we're trying to discuss. Your emotions can and will ebb and flow. If you can find a way to quiet your thoughts, to get your thoughts and emotions out of the way, even through momentary meditation, you will find me and our connection in your deepest and truest feelings. There you will find what was so elusive yesterday. We just want a few physical signposts available to guide you to a quiet moment where things can come back into focus. In the deepest eternal terms, there can be no doubt that we are always and forever connected in our perfect love. This connection is always there whether you remember it or not.

If we took the time, we would find what triggered your awful day yesterday. Instead, let's use that energy to enjoy this moment. Detective work won't fix anything since there really wasn't anything wrong.

I know you don't want to feel that way ever again, but realize fearing that you might is what will bring about what it is you fear. I'll say it again, I still exist, and I still love you. This is our eternal truth. I know you will have moments or possibly even days of doubt, but that doesn't change a thing. It can't. It is not possible.

I know you don't doubt my love., so let that be the place to start. Find things that remind you of my love, things that are so loud they scream at you. The wall of pictures you've made of our time in St. Lucia is a wonderful place to start. You can see it from your chair even while you're watching TV.

Another thing to remember is how all of the medication you take to control your physical pain dulls your ability to be aware of me. They can also encourage a little bit of your depression to return. It's unlikely you'll sink to where you were after your second surgery, but It's an important thing to keep in mind.

Do not trust your emotions trust me. Really trust me particularly when you're down. Who else understands you and loves you enough to reach across time and space?

Remember how much time it took after we were together for you to realize and accept that you could even be loved? You didn't believe in love without strings attached until you realized that is how you loved me.

Finally, you came to know that if you had the capacity to love another soul so purely, that I could possibly have the same love for you. You saw my faults and flaws. You knew my fears, and all my shortcomings. It's not that you didn't care about or see those things, they simply didn't matter. You didn't overlook them or look past them; you just accepted them and accepted me exactly as I was. That was pure, perfect, unconditional love. It seemed like it took you forever to accept the same love could exist from me. Well, it did feel like forever, but you finally got there.

Our current situation is somewhat similar. While you no longer doubt our love, it's hard to buck human nature. As children, it was drilled into our heads that only certain people would find God's love, only the righteous would enjoy eternity. The rest of us, well, we were screwed. Forever separate not only from God, but everyone we loved. There was this spiritual jujitsu involved so no one could ever be sure where they stood.

This system that counted on doubt and fear is the greatest barrier you and I now face. It is your childhood beliefs that are getting in the way. I want to be crystal clear about this. This barrier is a problem that you and I face. I do not mean to say that all or any specific religion or belief is evil or wrong. It is specifically for you and me in our way.

You, Tim, must let go of the doubt. It comes between us. Don't get caught up in judging anyone else's belief as it may be the best, possibly the only way for them, for their soul's path.

Look around you. There is nothing in your life that supports anything but the fact of my existence. You live in a house I found for you. I saved it, there's no other reason it was on the market for so long at the price it was listed at other than I wanted to live on this Desert Estate with you. You have Bear. We talked about you needing a dog for weeks; I found him 200 miles away! The facts around him are all synchronous miracles. There's no other explanation for him being with you, except that he and I conspired in Eternal time to get your friend back to you. There is absolutely no reasonable explanation for the car you're driving, except I found it for you. It's not that special, but try to explain how you're driving a $5,000 car that you bought for $2,500. It's my favorite make, Pontiac. Then explain the flowers and seashells you found in the driver's glove box, that is our car, plain and simple.

You do live in a world of miracles because you live in our world of perfect love. What we had, what others saw, continues. It hasn't become restricted by my passing. The loss of my body has allowed access to the fullness of eternity.

What you saw as you were dozing off last night is an accurate depiction. You saw an ancient Japanese gazebo built with only precision joints in the wood, no nails or fasteners of any kind. That gargantuan puzzle is how our life together has been and will continue to be, interlocked in countless hidden places, strong beyond measure. The storm may clear the cherry blossoms from the branches of the nearby trees, but the structure remains. Our love is immortal. Look for the proof in everything and everywhere.

Your Eternal Love

"You do live in a world of miracles because you live in our world of perfect love. What we had, what others saw, continues. It hasn't become restricted by my passing. The loss of my body has allowed access to the fullness of eternity."

18

Play with Bear

May 12, 2021, 5:20 a.m.

The day after the fourth anniversary of Mari Lynn's passing, I began to write a letter to her. I was interrupted several times.

--Tim--

My Love,

Why am I not able to be with you? I want to come home so very badly. It seems there is absolutely no purpose for me to still be here. There is no one who would really miss me. Yes, I know there are many people who have much worse situations, but why am I still here? What's the point of all of this suffering? Four years ago today, I woke up for the first time in an empty house. I miss you terribly. I need you for so many reasons. Just as I feel like life is getting better for me, something happens that reminds me you're gone and I'm simply by myself. I worked so hard and focused so much on getting to the beach. I ignored my exercises, and my feet are painful enough that I can't put my shoes on. The house is a mess. I don't have the energy to take care of it. My body hurts so much I have to choose between simple things that should all get done. What could possibly be the purpose for having to live this way. I really need that question answered. I can't keep up, I'm overwhelmed with everything. I…

Mari Lynn Interrupting,

Oh, My Love,

I get it, I really do. You're feeling overwhelmed. This feeling will pass. There is not much I could say right now, except I love you and I am holding you. I understand what it feels like while you are by yourself and that is all you can see, but you are not alone. That would be impossible, because I am right here. I know the past few days have been full of the memories of four years ago. Yesterday you tried to fill the day with activities to keep your mind busy, but the consequences of that are that your body is in extra pain that takes you even lower. Take a break for the next few days to let your body rest. Play with Bear, feed the kittens, exercise your body. Spend a little time at the beginning and end of each day in meditation. Do these simple things for a little while and you'll begin to have less pain.

--Tim--

My pain is bad enough that I can feel this pen scratching the paper with my back. It's quite excruciating and...

-- Mari Lynn interrupting--

Shift your weight a bit. Take a moment and watch the sunrise color the mountains, and yes, take a pill even though it's only 6 a.m. It wasn't long ago that was the first thing you had to do every morning. While this pain seems pretty severe, and more than you can bear, remember we have endured much, much worse. You are struggling more than you need to and you are stronger than you think. While all this discomfort feels overwhelming, it will soon pass. The fact that you have enough faith to be here in our front room with a pen and paper tells me you will be okay. I know the house is a mess and I know how that makes you anxious. I know you're feeling behind on everything, but there's hardly anything that has an actual schedule. Call Mark and get an extension on our taxes. Do that today and get it out of your head for the next few months. Other than that, there's literally nothing that has to be done. So, play with Bear, feed the kittens, do your exercises, and I promise you your body will soon be feeling well enough to get to the things that are overwhelming you.

As far as why you are still here and not home with me, well, the answer will soon present itself. I know that is not what you wanted to hear and it's not satisfying, but you must listen. You are not alone; I live in our house with you; you can be by yourself, however, it is not possible for you to ever be alone. I get that you feel alone, especially around significant days like yesterday. I promise, there is a future when these days will be looked forward to as much as a child looks forward to Christmas morning. For today, however, put one foot in front of the other. Play with Bear, feed the kittens, and do your physical exercise. Maybe add some time floating in our pool. Soon you'll become open to the joy this home we bought together has to offer. Today is Tuesday. Take a break at least through the weekend. I promise you'll be feeling better by then.

How your body feels is tied tightly to how your emotions are going and vice versa. If you get down, your body responds with more pain. If you overexert and are in physical pain, your emotions will sink. Why do you think that is? Figuring this question out is part of our eternal journey. Of course, you're right, I could just tell you. That solution would be simple, but your knowing would not be as deep as if you worked it out. I'm not saying you have to learn this lesson all by yourself.

But gaining this knowledge needs to be a journey of discovery, much the same way that you came to the conclusion that our beach trip was not going to happen.

For the past few months, I've been leading you to understand that while going to the beach would be fantastic, it would be okay if it didn't happen. I wasn't slowly letting you down so your disappointment wouldn't be so great. No, I was both encouraging you to get to the beach to have an enjoyable time and leading you to understand that in order to have a good time at the beach, or anywhere, for that matter, you must bring that joy with you. If you don't have it here, you can't suddenly find it on vacation. We never went anywhere to find our joy or our bliss. It followed us! Yes, our physical bodies found rest and relaxation away from the grind of our daily lives, but how many times did we come home from a restful vacation more physically tired than when we left?

--Tim—

This is sort of weird, but I just realized I'm feeling much better. My body still hurts. I can't tell you how uncomfortable it is to feel this pen scratching the paper with my lower back, but just coming here seems…

--Mari Lynn interrupting again--

To have helped? Of course, it helps, Silly. This is our sanctuary, our safe place in this physical world. You pushed so hard for actual months to go to the beach for just four nights. All that physical and emotional effort, not to mention all the money, only to find out you didn't need to be there to find your rest.

--"What a Wonderful World" by Israel Kamakawiwoʻole (1988) begins to play as my music stream seems to become louder--

--Tim--

I still don't know how you pull this off. (Referring to the music)

--Mari Lynn--

It's very complex. Time and physics you know, but you're worth it. It's actually easier than sleeping on a hospital floor for ten days, but I'd do both every day for the rest of your life. Here in the physical world, by the way, sleeping on the floor was very hard on my body but it was the easiest decision I've ever made. I know you understand what I'm saying. I saw how difficult taking care of me was for those 15 months. It saddened me so much to see your physical pain. But I also knew how easy it was for you to do it.

--My memory takes me back to the months of Mari Lynn's illness. In an instant, I recall the physical demands on my body as I cared for her needs, but in the same moment, I'm filled with gratitude for the opportunity to return loving kindness to the one who (for twentw-two years) had given so much of herself to me. --

It's much like now. It breaks my heart to see you struggle, but it also makes my soul soar to be the one holding you. I have so much faith in you and in us. Just know that your journey will lead you home with me, but there's still so much beauty along the way for us to experience. Do not allow the loss of my body to get in our way. We are together and experiencing each new and exciting moment together as one.

Your Eternal Love

"Just know that your journey will lead you home with me, but there's still so much beauty along the way for us to experience. Do not allow the loss of my body to get in our way. We are together ..."

19

Rocketship of Love

In February and March 2022, Mari Lynn's brother and I took an extended vacation. He wanted to go to the Daytona 500 for his 60th birthday. The three of us had planned this trip for Mari Lynns 60th, but we could not go since she passed away shortly before her 58th birthday. With him driving and me navigating, we traveled over 7000 miles in five weeks in my motorhome. We went to the 500, spent time at my dad's home in Orlando, Florida, with a cousin of mine in Tennessee, and nearly a week with my family in Colorado Springs before going to the NASCAR race in Las Vegas, and finally home.

Our time in Colorado was amazing. John loved it and asked me to please bring him whenever I planned my next visit. If I ever needed a driver, he was my man.

The true highlight of the entire trip was an evening at the Olive Garden restaurant. My Colorado family consists of five of our children and their spouses and (at the time) ten grandchildren, all granddaughters between the ages of two and 21. Thankfully, the restaurant provided a separate room with two tables. I sat at the head of one table with an empty chair next to me and a place setting for Mari Lynn. To complete her table setting, I ordered a glass of her favorite wine. After I came back from chatting with ten beautiful young ladies, there, by Mari Lynn's wine glass, were items that each adult child happened to carry with them. Out of purses and pockets came the photos, toys, and trinkets my children had with them to remind them of their mom. I added a small urn of her ashes I was carrying on my vacation. Spontaneously, we had created a memorial service.

For the first time, I decided to tell them why Mari Lynn and I had made such a huge decision that had affected their lives in such a profound way. I gave them a little of the adult version. I told them about the risk we saw for them if we had allowed their lives to be formed by our childhood religion and deeply flawed first marriages and told them that *they* were the only reason Mari Lynn, and I were ever together. Finally, I was able to tell them that my first wife keeping our daughter's violation a secret from me was the cause of that marriage failing. I also explained how we were willing to accept the story everyone else told of us leaving our old lives for only a passionate physical attraction, a story that had given us cover for our true passion—them. After a few minutes of reiterating why their seemingly happy memories in their "first families" were actually headed towards a generational and perpetual nightmare, I apologized for not being able to keep up with being the kind of father and grandfather I wanted to be. It seemed to me that when Mari Lynn passed, so did much of my ability to be in their lives.

My oldest daughter stood up and with tears streaming down her face said," You don't get it, do you? As adults with challenges of our own, we saw what you guys did and understood. Look at these two tables. You did this! You made us feel safe and let us make our own decisions about who we would become. You made us feel loved.

Mari Lynn was such a strong woman. She wasn't my birth mother, but from the first day she loved me as her own. She was my mom, my momma. She showed me so much and I'm so grateful to have had her in my life; but you must know, none of this would have happened without you."

March 12, 2022, 6 a.m.

My Love,

I'm always so happy when you begin your day with me in this way. I know you know I'm always here, but you also know I'm with you all day long all night long for that matter. I'm glad you're getting rest from our trip. What an exciting time we had! Those few days with our kids and our granddaughters was so very special to me. I know you felt it too.

It was wonderful for you to see what I've known since the day I passed. We did good, better than good! Better than we had any expectation of. What we accomplished in a single generation is not normal. It is a direct result of that January day in 1995, when we hatched a crazy plan to show six children what love can really do when it's allowed to be shown in perfection. Our absolute love for them was the driving force behind our entire time together. It still is. I know it's very easy for you to not see. You're so far away from them. I know you feel that distance in more than simply miles.

You think you are not being the kind of father or grandfather you think they diserve. When are you going to believe people's word about how much you are loved? Every one of them would do anything for you.

It's true because they each felt you risked everything for them. Their love for you is real, deep, and forever.

I recognize your history on how loved you feel does not help. Your view of how lovable you are is very distorted. You did not get a clear picture of how love is supposed to work and from a very early age, you understood love to be only a behavior. Well, it is not. To realize this truth, it took you recognizing how much you were willing to give up to protect Joanna. You had no words, no vocabulary for the deep feelings you had. Your righteous anger towards your cousin and your willingness to do anything for Joanna was a doorway into what you know love to be today.

When you told me about how things in your life had fallen apart, about how you'd completely failed all of your children especially Joanna, I did not see a failed parent telling me of the things that had made life unbearable. No, I saw a father who recognized how he was willing to burn the whole world he knew to the ground in order to protect his children. You did not know the language of love, but you knew to the deepest part of your soul how to love.

I saw a true father, and that was what gave me the strength to do the same for my girls. You thought I was the one who showed you how to love, but look back with my eternal eyes. See those first moments clearly. It was you who showed me what pure and perfect love was. How far you were willing to go for Joanna was inspiration for me to be brave enough to leave a very destructive marriage.

The world saw this event, the beginning of our lives together as my physically seducing you, but it was the other way around. Your absolute love for your daughter is what, in an instant, seduced me. It was so intoxicating to be around love so strong.

It's true I had quietly hoped against hope that we would find a way to be together. You thought that our first coffee was about me holding you up through the greatest crisis you could possibly imagine. The reality was, I was not holding you, but holding on to the rocket ship of unconditional love that sat before me believing that he was a failure as a father.

Do you not now see what we did together, what we have accomplished, is not because I comforted you, but because you showed me that true love, perfect love, does not look for safe harbor? It propels itself into the storm. It does not look to subdue the storm; it sees through it, knowing that without a storm, love can never be proven to a world longing for safe harbor.

For nearly 30 years, you have had this concept completely backward, and again, you are having the same

reversed view of love. The father and grandfather concept you have of yourself is very flawed. Your children do not see you as needing uplifted by their love.
You are the solid rock their love is and has always been
anchored to. Your view of our family's love has the cart
so far in front of the horse, the horse thinks he is all
alone.

You are not alone. You are so far from alone, not
just because I'm still in your life, but because you have
an entire army of kids and grandkids who would decide
to burn their own world to the ground in a heartbeat because they actually saw you do it for them.

I know you do not feel adequate, that somehow, when
I passed away, most of our parenting and grand parenting also died. What you fail to realize is that you were
always the fuel and the engine for this family that was
built on love. Did you not hear Joanna? You are far
better at this than you think.

Did your early life make it more difficult to see this
truth? Absolutely, but it did not close you off to love
itself. It is true, your vocabulary was stunted, but that in
no way limited the depth of your ability to love and be
loved that has been cultivated over eons.

In case you have not gotten it yet, love is your soul's
work; it is our work. You express love through many

gifts: healing, knowing, seeing, and hearing; but the way all of our work has been (or will be) accomplished is through love.

Your Eternal Love

"True love, perfect love, does not look for safe harbor? It propels itself into the storm. It does not look to subdue the storm; it sees through it, knowing that without a storm, love can never be proven to a world longing for safe harbor."

20

We Knew

March 24, 2022, 6:24 a.m.

My Love,

You are really something. I mean that in the best, most loving way possible. You are so close to finally realizing some of the potential I saw in you all those years ago. While I did not possess the vocabulary or even the understanding of what might be possible for you if you really connected to source, I could see from our first meeting how special you were. Jim and Marcos also saw something in you that first day we all met in that church classroom. Of course, I had no idea, no way to possibly see the future, but from those first moments, I knew our story had just started. You and I were on a collision course with this moment in March (2022) on a clear desert morning over 30 years later.

I know how reluctant you are to find a public voice in all of this awakening that's occurring to you, but that is not and should not be a consideration in this process at all. You are beginning to recognize and accept who you are and who you have been for many lifetimes. This concept is not new for either of us. I have loved you, literally, since time began. We have been together through every possible human experience. There is truly nothing we have not done together, no mountain we have not climbed.

When we first met, there was a compatibility and comfort that seemed simultaneously new and ancient. In a fraction of a moment, two people who had never met, instantly were aware of each other on a level that only one's spirit knows.

In the first few years, we allowed ourselves to continue with our life's path as individuals. However, as it became more and more obvious, first to me, then to others, and finally to you, the part of our being that lived in that ancient space was becoming dominant. We found ourselves being drawn to each other by forces as great as gravity. There would be no denying our souls' chosen path.

The circumstances that allowed us to be together were as pure as could possibly be formulated by a watchful universe. Once our awakening reached terminal velocity, and once our eyes became open to the earthly path we had been on, it was obvious we had to act. We found righteous cause our children were at risk both physically and emotionally. Our parental example was one of accepting abuse and (in a passive way) promoting a broken view of love. Our failure became crystal clear and thus, the final righteous justification for us to alter our course towards our true soul's path. We accepted every judgment: We had chosen to leave our earthly path, our families, and our church for a simple physical relationship. While we absolutely did revel in our newfound experience of physical love, it was not the cause of our being together, but a byproduct of our choice to give our children a safe place to find their own way. To this day, there are people who look at our choices and think our decisions were based purely on physical desire. That view has the cart so far before the horse you would think it's a horseless carriage (laughing). See, even during serious discussions, I can still tell a little joke.

Anyway, this is a long way to say that on a soul level, we knew from that first brief meeting, that on a clear desert morning in March almost 30 years later, this moment would come to pass.

All of the circumstances of the first three years, and all of the drama of the following five years, led us to a place where we could withstand the pressure that came from a life-altering injury. The lessons of loving strength and perseverance we provided our children will now encourage a wider audience. The world will now begin to see how our earthly life that followed our soul's path has always caused the entire universe to dance even while we were literally struggling to find a way for you to walk (laughing). See, jokes.

What is on our horizon is a beautiful conclusion to all of the hard work, all of the challenges we endured. We chose to take a righteous journey instead of the path of least resistance. We can now share the beautiful anguish of the blessings and challenges we endured for the sole benefit of six souls.

At the time, the example we intentionally set was only focused on the six. As they grew older and married, our target audience expanded, and the beauty of birth began to occur. We are now blessed with ten granddaughters. And while our children did not escape their early formative years without injury, they all view their scars as well-earned in the light of the struggle between love and fear. All of our granddaughters are profoundly better off than we could have ever believed possible when on another clear day we chose to live in love.

Your Eternal Love

"We have been together through every possible human experience. There is truly nothing we have not done together, no mountain we have not climbed."

21

Perfect Papers

It was summer and I was trying to get my RV ready for a month long trip with Mari Lynn's brother to the Daytona 500 in February. That may not sound like a very challenging task, but it seemed like everything on our 15-year-old motorhome needed either repaired or replaced. Where I live, the month of August is hot, extremely hot. Temperatures can easily be over 100 degrees by 9 a.m. and top out at over 115 degrees. In addition, my ability to be active was limited by my injury that, even though it happened over 20 years before, still demanded that I spend most of my day in a recliner with my feet up. Between the heat and my health, I was only able to work two or three hours a day. Even with six months to go, I felt like I wasn't going to get everything done.

In the middle of all this preparation, I got a call from our youngest daughter, Jessica, who was now the mother of three beautiful girls. Her first marriage had failed, and the children's father was taking them for Spring Break. She and her second husband suddenly realized they had a week to themselves. Her mom, Donna, had heard the news and had "suggested" they spend it with her in San Diego.

As our kids were growing up, they each seemed to find spouses whose parents had divorced. Now our granddaughters were growing up with three other sets of grandparents who all were demanding to be *the* grandparents. There was competition to be the ones to take them on their first visit to Disneyland, every trip to the zoo or beach, and even the ones to host birthdays. Mari Lynn and I could see the pressure these new parents were under and made a conscience decision not to add to it. When we would get visits, they were often only a day or two added onto a week with the other grandparents. Every time, our kids would thank us for not putting them in the middle of the fight over who would be the favorite grandma. While it was hard seeing social media posts of everyone else having days at Disneyland and such, we knew we were doing the right thing. Oddly, over time it seemed our strategy was unexpectedly winning a fight from which we had graciously withdrawn.

When our daughter called to tell me that she and her new husband had a week off, but that they needed to fly to her mom's house, I wasn't surprised. I was thrilled though, when she told me that they would be driving the five hours from San Diego to spend a day or so with me. They would be here in less than a week and the house cleaning had been neglected. I had been so focused on the RV, I had barely taken the time to wash the dishes. I dropped every other task and for three days focused solely on getting the house ready for visitors. Their visit only lasted about 24 hours.

August 10, 2021, 6:13 a.m.

My Dearest Love,

I can sense how lonely you feel. I can and do experience everything you do, so please know that I'm right next to you now. It was such a wonderful thing to have our daughter and her husband here for a few short hours. I know how much you worked and put your normal things aside for a one-day visit. I know how you feel like letting the RV work take a backseat puts pressure on you, but most of all, I know how having such a short visit can actually make you feel even more isolated. I get it, but think a little more about what was accomplished in 24 hours.

Jessica now has a better understanding about your daily life, and you have a far better idea of how the decisions of our early time together in this lifetime made it possible for her to find her own happiness. Of course, Jessica has had her own struggles, and her journey has not always been smooth, but look at her now. Our investments have paid a very large dividend. She has no idea of how our childhood belief system works. Jessica was so young when our life together began, that a great deal of how we each were raised as children never really sunk in; it never really took. The older kids have memories of that stifling belief system and how our families had distorted even the few eternal truths that were included in our upbringing.

This is fantastic news for you, so don't let yourself get down about such a short visit. I know it may seem painful, as these quick visits seem to be all you get. You must know that the decisions we made over 25 years ago have allowed each of our children to find their own eternal path. They are no longer stuck being raised in almost the exact same way as our great-grandparents.

I get that you miss our children, and short visits can make you feel worse, but they live that far away for a reason. We were able to give them all they needed by giving them such a loving and truly unconditional way to form their own beliefs.

Your visit was so short because we are still the ones that refuse to put pressure on them. We make no demands on their time. Jessica came to visit because she loves you more than anything, but she had to leave because others still demand her time.

This is our continued sacrifice for all of our children. Our love is pure enough that we don't make those demands, and it's this unconditional love Jessica is raising her three daughters with.

I know you feel like you've again lost something, but think long and hard about the word, "sacrifice". When anything is done by choice in pure, perfect, and unconditional love the word, "sacrifice" doesn't really apply. You gave up nothing and gained everything. Where you and I exist, time is sort of irrelevant. Since all you feel you missed out on with her was time, then absolutely nothing was lost. Look at what was gained: You were given a huge confirmation that our decisions, as radical and sometimes painful as they were at the time, really paid off for her. Jessica is where she is in this moment because we were willing to make very hard choices. When you look at it this way, "sacrifice" is a really bad choice of words.

So, as with anything, try to see with my eternal eyes. We still need to have a long view. Don't just focus on a few moments. Look at all we have gained. A gift cannot be viewed as a sacrifice. So, sort of get over it! (laughing)

--At this moment, a small house finch came and spent several moments looking at me, sitting on the sill of the picture window. --

--Tim--

Thanks for helping me get back to at least seeing where center is. Oh, and thanks for the bird. You know I love it when you do that.

--Mari Lynn--

You know you're very easy for me to get to, so don't be surprised when I send you something physical, like a bird or a dragon fly or a freshening breeze when I know you need a little pick me up. If you pay more attention, you'll see a lot more of those things are happening all the time.

Now, to get back on track, spend a little time this afternoon and make that list we talked about a couple of weeks ago. It will help a lot when you have to take breaks in getting the RV ready for our February road trip, or in our landscaping projects, or getting the property ready for your mom to live here. I know it feels like there's a lot that will be on that list, but there really isn't. A list will help you prioritize your schedule. Yes, if you want, put the whole thing on a spreadsheet and I'll help you manage it.

You know I'm around all day long. All night for that matter. I'm a 24/7 kind of deal. You can't get away from me even if you wanted to. (laughing)

I know you and can easily see how much you want to be near me. What you often forget is how much of a two-way street that longing is. While this time after one of us has passed may look from the outside like we are separate, you and I both know that's nowhere near true.

If you allow yourself to focus on the things that we seem to have lost, it could get quite overwhelming. While it's okay to recognize we no longer have the benefit of physical touch, you must simultaneously recognize that nothing was lost. We simply moved that physical contact and expanded it into something much better. These short moments in time, when one of us has returned to our natural state and one remains physical, are the moments when the most spectacular eternal growth takes place. When we are both physical, our daily life experience can easily take up our entire view and eternal growth can be slow. If we are both in spirit, it's a time to review what we've learned. Think of it more like a period of looking at our work and grading our tests. Naturally, we always have perfect papers. (laughing) We also use time in spirit to plan what comes next on the physical plane; but how we exist right now, one in spirit and one still physical, is the moment when our eternal growth explodes.

Our desire to be together is absolute and drives us to find each other. The dynamics of where we find ourselves right now, allow the best of both sides of the Great Barrier. In these moments, nothing stands between us and nothing extends beyond us. In these moments, we can know the infinite and still smell the fragrance of the roses we are growing. Yes, we are having our eternal cake and eating it too; but if you look closely, it's a cake that we ourselves baked.

This is our continued bliss: To know eternal existence in all its fullness and to continue to be one.

Your Eternal Love

"If you allow yourself to focus on the things that we seem to have lost, it could get quite overwhelming. While it's okay to recognize we no longer have the benefit of physical touch, you must simultaneously recognize that nothing was lost. We simply moved that physical contact and expanded it into something much better."

22

Our Story

June 5, 2022, 6:39 a.m.

My Love,

I know it has been several days since you sat here with
me with the intention of writing my thoughts, but you know
in a very deep and profound way that I'm with you every
moment of every day. Even when you are not aware of
me, I am here not lurking in some misty shadow, but right
by your side helping you throughout your day.

I know there are times you get distracted. There are
moments when you allow life to be too big for you to
focus on the many small things that I do to call your
attention to me and to our continuing life together. I know
there are changes going on in your life right now. You
are becoming more and more aware of the gifts you have
possessed in one form or another for eons. Early in

our time together, I saw these spiritual abilities and tried to encourage you to strengthen them. At the time, we did not have the depth of spiritual vocabulary or the life experience to realize what all of those gifts could become. In a comparatively secular life, I simply knew you had an ability to hear more than what someone was saying and could see more than with just your eyes. Life experience of spirit and this world of afterlife communication was never required until I passed away.

My transition into Spirit would cause a gap in our time together if we did not act. We always thought we had been together before, and so it followed that we would be together again. We had a quiet hope that we would find a way to be together if one of us transitioned without the other.

When I became ill, this quiet hope moved to the front burner. It became all important as we immediately, even before a doctor's diagnosis, knew I was going to pass away. Even with that knowledge, we did not despair. We just suddenly knew we would find a way. We were so confident, so sure that we found it unnecessary to discuss or even make plans on how to make it work. We simply and absolutely knew it would.

Without knowing, you began to hear me weeks before I passed. I was able to hear you guiding me from the world of Spirit as your eternal essence reassured me of our timeless spiritual connection. It was your voice that guided me as you reminded me of who I am and of who we are. What I'm reminding you of is how we began our current way of communicating before I passed completely into Spirit.

After I passed, who do you think it was who told you that to find me, you needed to return to where our spiritual awakening began this lifetime? It was the book <u>Conversations with God</u> (Conversations with God, An Uncommon Dialogue, Book 1, 1995) which jumpstarted our transition from our childhood beliefs that were so narrow and would not allow any communication after death, let alone what and how we are doing this right now. We were told being able to talk to dead people was not real, that it was a trick of Satan, and a way to fast track yourself to damnation.

Do not lament our childhood and early adult life as wasted time. There were obvious things in it that were simply wrong, but they were the first cobblestones in "the broken road that led us straight" to this moment where it's possible to write the thoughts of someone whose body did die over five years ago.

As you look back on our time together, this lifetime, you will see many moments when our spiritual growth accelerated. From our teenage years until we met, we both in various ways questioned our ingrained belief system. We both had a deep longing that our parents' religion could not fulfill. We both had quietly given up hope of ever finding the missing piece of our lives. We both married because that is "what you are supposed to do" and still could not find the missing piece. We both thought this longing was a normal part of life.

I recognized what was missing the moment I saw you in that church classroom. I was shocked but quietly relieved when my reaction to seeing you was an audible gasp that I was sure someone must have heard. Jennifer Shaffer was right. That moment for me was a moment of pure elation and simultaneously an "Oh shit!" moment, as I fully saw what would fulfill my deepest longing and knew I would never have what was required to fill it. For the most part, you seemed outwardly oblivious, however I saw your reaction as our souls made contact. You could not bear to look. I saw you momentarily stare at me with the gaze of eternity. You tried to immediately look away, but in that moment, in that small instant, you saw the longing of your deepest heart fulfilled.

It took years and so many twists and turns in both of our lives for us to find ourselves at that La Canada coffee shop on a January afternoon in 1995, when our souls' longing met with our life decisions. In less than seven weeks we were living together, and rescuing our children from the spiritual confusion of our childhoods. And in less than a year, we were singing our own song in a mountain chapel in front of our friends and family.

This is a story that I will never get tired of telling, but as it's recounted, notice all of the moments of profound change. Take the time to remember the feelings that surrounded these times of transition. We often embraced the changes as joyous occasions, however there were some that caused a lot of uncertainty. Remember how stressed we were trying to find a home to rent in Glendale? That is, until all of a sudden, the right home in the right location with the right landlord seemed to fall from Heaven. Remember how distressed we were when a drunk driver came down our street and totaled both of our cars, and how unhappy I was with the car we were able to afford, until we realized that it was the perfect car for you to ride in after your injury? That injury had not yet taken place when the universe forced us to trade in my favorite car.

If you look, you will not be able to find one single challenge in our life that, at the moment, seemed catastrophic, but was in reality, another stone paving our broken road. By the time of my illness, we had learned that rocks blocking us were in fact steppingstones, and this continues to be true.

In the place we find ourselves right now, we are again in transition. You are finding your spiritual voice, a voice I've heard since the day we first briefly met nearly 30 years ago. Remember the lessons of those years and be unconcerned. I've heard you loud and clear.

I know your only true fear in this life you now live is losing me. Look back on our life. Look at all the times I fought just to be with you. Look at all of the years I spent in quiet patience, longing for you, waiting for you to realize that you longed for me too. Think of all the ways I protected you from the storms life was sending our way. I stood with you through times of pain that others found too great. I slept on hospital floors, not once, but three times. I pushed you in a wheelchair; I drove you to hundreds of physical therapy appointments, and even more doctor's appointments. Think about it. If I was willing to do all of that, how deep do you think my love for you is? Do you think I would allow something as small as the loss of my body to come between us?

I do know your fear, and I know better than you where it comes from. We have been through so much this lifetime, but we've had countless lifetimes of love. For me to not be with you is simply not possible. I leave you small signs all day long. I'm with you every night in your dreams. You can actually feel my essence as my life force interacts with your body. We talk about everything all day long, and you can pick up a pen and take dictation for me as I give you encouragement from the other side of the thinning veil.

All of these experiences say the simplest of things I exist. I love you more than you could possibly know, and I will never ever leave you.

Your Eternal Love

"Even when you are not aware of me, I am here not lurking in some misty shadow, but right by your side helping you throughout your day."

Conclusion

So why did I feel compelled to write this book? I have had people suggest that there was a more "acceptable" way for us to start our lives together. However, they do not take into account the danger we were in from Marcos who had publicly threatened to kill Mari Lynn, her daughters, and me. They did not live with a man who in the months before we escaped had been sitting in the dark for hours every night with a revolver, spinning the cylinder and pulling the trigger over and over. There were genuine threats from a man who, over a year after Mari Lynn had left him, was still so angry he wrote a letter detailing what would happen to us if we ever entered the city of Burbank. He threatened, "They will never find your bodies!"

If we had tried to separate from our spouses and wait for our divorces to be final, both of our families would have pressured us to come back. Our church would have done everything it could to force us back to the cookie cutter life that was crushing us. A committee of church elders told us that so long as our outward lives were that of upstanding church members, what we did in private was our business. The elders shocking suggestion that living a lie was okay with God made our decision easy and, we declined their offer to return. They immediately removed our names from the church books, a proceeding in our church that is similar to excommunication. A clean break was the *only* healthy and sane choice open to us.

We had been living an outward life that seemed righteous. We were busy doing the "right" thing with inward lives that were at best empty and sometimes terrifying. We were willing to burn our own world to the ground if it meant that our six children had the simple choice to become who *they* wanted to be. Our children's well-being became our guiding principle, our North Star. There is not one situation or decision given the same information we had at the time, that we would have done differently.

Of course, there were times when life seemed overwhelming, like what we had decided to put ourselves through was costing too much. For the most part, only one of us experienced these low moments at a time. In the years after my injury, I did experience severe clinical depression. There were times the pressure of keeping a family business afloat was almost more than Mari Lynn could bear. There were times the craziness our exes put us through made us want to disappear. But our ever-present concern for our children's futures kept us fighting for every inch of life and love we could hold. During these times of difficulty we began to notice the most incredible thing. The one of us that seemed to be holding up the one in crisis was actually being uplifted by the one who was down.

As I reflect on the time we were physically in each other's lives, I realize the eternal connection Mari Lynn and I share is uncommon. As I look back, *what* made us different was that we quickly realized that death does not exist. While we didn't yet have the correct words, we absolutely knew we had shared countless lifetimes. Since we knew that was true, it seemed only logical to conclude there would be countless more. We were in the *middle* of an eternal love story. Because we believed those things, we learned to have absolutely no fear of death. It was sort of a superpower. It made what we were challenged with, just that, challenges. A joyous way for us to declare our love to the universe. We knew we would find a way to be together if we were separated by a thinning veil. We had no idea *how* this would happen but fully expected it *to* happen.

I know it sounds a little trite, but we learned that through love, anything really *is* possible. We found that the love for our children gave us the strength and perseverance to leave toxic marriages and warped religious dogma that had been twisted so far from its original truth that it was completely unrecognizable, *and* we found we could bring six children with us. Every one of them is where they are because they chose it and the next generation, our grandchildren, are profoundly better off than we ever believed possible.

Since Mari Lynn passed away, another truth I've learned is that the love needed to overcome challenges does not need to be earthbound. The still small voice, our intuition, that gut feeling is often our loved ones reaching across the thinning veil guiding us through our challenges towards our greatest joy.

When I started writing this book, a couple of realizations became clear: First, there's a significant difference when Mari Lynn writes through me (my hand moves much faster than my mind), and the second idea that came to me was that many of our letters needed context that would result in a story instead of just a compilation of letters.

The most profound thing I know is that what we are doing since Mari Lynn transitioned to her natural state is available in one form or another to anyone. There are signs all around us if we open ourselves and do not judge or demand they appear in a particular way. "*If you're only looking for rainbows, you may not see the sunset.*" We are proof that nothing is lost, that love extends beyond time and space.

This project has been overwhelming at times in the most extraordinary way. I've written about *some* of the challenges we faced and shared only *a few* of the miracles. There is no way to contain in one book our entire lives together from meeting in a church classroom in 1990, until now, over 6 years after her body died; but in trying to do just that, I've had the extraordinary experience of remembering and reliving all of it and for that we are deeply grateful.

PS:

My Eternal Love says, "*To be continued.*"

February 9, 2021

One evening, I was so tired that I asked Mari Lynn to help me sleep until 6 a.m. I woke up at 5:55 a.m.

I went out to start the coffee and get set up in my front room reading chair. As I was walking through the living room I thought, or more precisely, I was told to take the camera with me; the sunrise was going to be really spectacular.

With the camera in hand, I looked out the front picture window and saw a brilliant sunrise with all the pink, purple, orange, and red imaginable, but with one additional item. In all this color was the sliver of a crescent moon.

I hadn't even changed out of my night clothes; instead, I spent the next 40 minutes taking several hundred pictures. (Maybe one would be really awesome.)

The desert sunrise was so intense I had to ask Mari Lynn, "Do you see the sunrise?" Her answer came flooding over me.

"Of Course, I do!"

My Dearest Love,
Do you see this sunrise?

Of course, I do

Do you know my pain
and feel my fear?

Of course, I do

My Dearest One
Do you see where my joy has gone?
For I have lost it

Yes, My Love
Of course, I do

Love of my life
Do you know how lost I am?

Yes, My Dearest
Of course, I do

My Dearest Love
I see the sunrise because I sent it to you,
and I know your pain and fear for we are one soul

Oh, My Dearest One
You have not lost your joy
only set it aside
and you are not lost
I know where you are

I know these things
for though my body is gone
you are still my breath
I feel these things
though I cannot touch you
I still caress

You are my waking thought
as I am yours
My dreams at night
are only of you

Yes, Dearest Love
You've not one thought
that I do not know

So let me help you
and together we will find your joy

I know why you feel all these things
so let me answer
I am still here
I love you more than ever

Of course, I do

Tim & Mari Lynn Bair February 9, 2021

Tim Bair is a resident of Desert Hot Springs, California, where he resides on a four-acre property near Palm Springs. He leads a tranquil life, spending his days with his loyal German shepherd, Bear, and capturing the beauty of the desert landscape, flowers, and wildlife through his photography.

Despite facing personal hardships, Tim found his soulmate and demonstrated to their children that love can conquer all of life's challenges.

Tragically, Tim's beloved wife, Mari Lynn, passed away in 2017. However, he discovered that he could still communicate with her and began documenting their interactions. Their conversations flow effortlessly, as if they were still physically together.

For more information please visit our website: timbair6.com